Trapped in Poverty

An analysis of the misery of the Haitian People

Alix Michel

ISBN: 1482327708
ISBN-13: 9781482327700
Library of Congress Control Number: 2013902224
CreateSpace Independent Publishing Platform
North Charleston, South Carolina

Contents

Dedication

This book is dedicated to my family
Didi, Gerdley, Josh, and Gerlande

To my friends in Haiti
Marly and my cousin Jean Marie Victor (now deceased)
To my Brother Lionel Lamarre (now deceased)

To my old School classmates of
"Frere Polycarpe "and 'Frere Adrien"

To my old College comrades of "INAGHEI" of the 1980s

For all Caribbean's, Afro-Americans, Latino-Americans
and Asian-Americans I met in the libraries and
study rooms of Baruch & Brooklyn College.

For all my old teachers and Deans who have
influenced my Education

Warning

This book is the result of many hours of research conducted by the author. Staggered by the poverty level of his native country, he decided to investigate on the ground. It is not intended to support any political faction or client. It is an analysis of political and economical facts occurred in the past, compared to the present context with the intent to assess the future of things in that impoverished nation. By publishing the result of those studies we are not looking to harm anyone mentioned in that book. It is only our modest contribution in the struggle to save Haiti.

Preface

I write this book because I think that today Haiti needs ideas and advices from all his sons. I feel a special contemplation for those who sometimes take the risk to affirm their haitianhood abroad. I was blessed to attend Graduate School in Brooklyn College to put an end to a very long standing in the benches of School while studying the subject I like. Back in Haiti, when I started College at the National Institute of Administration-Management and International Studies (INAGHEI). I received my first notions with Professors Rony Durand & Edrice Vincent. Fascinated by the subject I started reading some French magazines sold in Haitian bookstores. Through the Editorials of Jean Daniel of "the new observer", Bechir Ben Yahmed, Senen Andriamirado and Sophie Bessis of "Young Africa", I cultured the jargon. To prepare a group term paper I had to read the "Capital "of Karl Marx and I discovered the other face of the Economic Science. Today, alongside of my regular job, I spend most of my time doing Economics research.

During the last years, I travelled often to Haiti, and I could observe in first place the nation scarcity level. This country is in a bad situation and I do not see clearly the exit sign. I consider the writing of this book as the payoff of a loan to it because the problems go profound into my heart. After each slippery the enemies of the nation are happy, because that confirms the thesis that nigger cannot lead a country on their own.

After many years of missing that event, I came back to visit the country for the carnival of 2008. Once outside the Airport, I felt shock by the environment of the country main entrance. On my way to the hotel, I saw desolation everywhere. The face of the people seems marked by their sufferings. When the carnival ended, I decided to make a tour of the City of my first childhood.

For two weeks, I toured Port au prince in taxis, tap tap, and by foot. I listened quietly to the people. I would like to compare the Haitian situation with a sick person knowing his sickness but unable to take care of it. Repudiated by the powers of the Western Hemisphere for claiming their liberty from slavery, betrayed by his own elites transformed now in oppressors, the Haitian people mostly adept of the Roman Catholic Church do not know what Saint to pray.

To move inside the town a half hour tour in the past has become a 90 minutes trip when there is no traffic. From 6 am, the long line of automobile blocks every road in the capital. One can barely breathe because of the gas coming from the engine pipes. Even on foot, it is not easy to move around the City. Streets merchants take over the sidewalks. Only the ability of the drivers prevents frequent road accidents.

What is referred in Economics as" informal Market" has taken over the legal shopping area. I questioned my cousin about their shopping place now; he answered to me: Delmas and PetionVille. At each street corner, amount of garbage piled up and many uncovered manholes. Next to that, stands a mobile restaurant (pap-padap) where people buy and eat their diner. Those who can pay the 10 gourdes (Haitian currency) to buy the dish are the lucky one compared to others who will spend the day without food. We found that in some quarters of the City, there are families who cannot afford to prepare a daily meal. We also discovered in some areas of the town that two or three families have to share their money in order to prepare a big dinner on Sundays.

People explained to us that the price of foods has skyrocketed during the last years and the few persons who have a job never had a salary increase.

Coming back from "La Plaine ", I took an autobus to Delmas. In front of me, I saw a person with a gun at his side. When he got off the car, I realized the one sitting next to me was wearing a gun also. When my cousin and I got off the Bus at Delmas 45, I said to him my fear. He reassured me not to worry because I am not a target. Who is a target I questioned him? A targeted person is someone who is in trouble with another. How many armed persons travel through the city and the countryside? The statistics is funny: 7000 police agents to secure a population of 10.000.000 of people. Eyes on his watch, it is four o'clock my cousin advised me, now we must go back to the hotel. It is very risky to walk in the streets at night. I had to return to New York the day after and I felt the desire to help my country.

I received the News of the Earthquake with a lot of apprehension. Images of Port au Prince from CNN uncovered the truth. A worldwide relief effort is organized to help Haiti. Port au Prince, Leogane, Petit Goave, and Jacmel were severely damaged. About 250.000 people were killed. Many offices building collapsed. The losses occurred were equal to the half of Haiti GDP. Many gatherings are organized worldwide to help the country. Corruption in the Haitian administration is well known; therefore, the international community demands that order must be restored.

Six months after the earthquake, I visited Haiti. The situation has become worst. The political instability orchestrated by the Preval administration is still going on. I want to offer my readers a flashback which will allow them to fully understand the present situation.

A democratic election was held in the country after the thirty years of the Duvalier dictatorship and the four years under military rulers. On December 16, 1990, the populists Aristide and Preval took power and no evident sign of future trouble was there. The former could not end his two mandates; the latter managed to finish his term anyway. However, economically both have failed the country. During the last twenty years, Haitian poverty has increased. Our population has grown under a 1.7% rate steadily and our economy has grown only at 1.1% rate. The high rate of mortality has prevented the population to increase more.

In the month of February 2001, Aristide was sworn in for the third time as Haiti president. At the same time, Gerard P Charles installed Gerard Gourgues as a parallel President in the country. The Lavalas regime was surprised and did not react immediately. In the following months, the group increased in number to attain 184 organizations. The murder of Armiot Metayer, one of Aristide henchmen happened in Gonaives. His fellow criminal accused Aristide to be behind the crime. All Gonaives stood behind the Metayer and the manifestation will last until Aristide departure in February 2004. Armed and financed by some invisible hands well known by spectators of the Haitian tragedy, Guy Philippe and Louis J Chamblain attacked the country on two fronts: the North and the Center. In less than ten years, Haiti was under occupation; this time the troops were from Brazil.

A de facto government with the head of the Haitian Supreme Court and a prime minister imported from abroad took power. The country went through a very sad period with daily kidnapping and murders. A new election is held and Rene Preval came back from retirement to lead the country. In the month of April 2008, to protest against an out of control inflation, the Haitian poor took the streets, and some were killed during the protest. The increase in the price of petrol and some basic foods for consumption has been transferred directly to the Haitian consumers. In the aftermath of the event, the Senate dismissed Prime Minister Jacques Alexis.

Michelle Pierre Louis took over as the new prime minister and the state of things began to change. During the summer of 2008, four hurricanes ripped through Haiti and the agricultural sector was devastated. Preval as always got rid of Michele P Louis as fast as possible. The January 12, 2010 earthquake surprised

Rene Preval and his government did not react promptly. As a result, he lost the confidence of the population. In spite of all, he was trying desperately to organize an election for his own successor. The international community, which holds the real power in Haiti, intervened and chose a popular singer.

I wanted to name this book "The Eternal misunderstanding "in memory of Jean Dominique, a journalist famous for his analyses of Haitian politics. He used this term very often to analyze the color problem in Haiti. For many Haitians scholars he was the messenger of the Haitian mulattoes. He advised the Jean Claude Duvalier regime to follow the path of the king Juan Carlos of Spain, who after the death of the dictator Francisco Franco succeeded in transforming Spain into a Democracy. The Haitian economy was booming at that time. No member of the government at that epoch would have listened to him because power for life meant to them wealth for life. He considered as a "Pyrrhic victory "what some proponents of that regime in Haiti celebrated as the 1946 Revolution. By listening to this radio commentator, many youngsters have realized the color problem in the country was a fake one. Unfortunately, he was murdered inside the radio-broadcast that made him famous.

I started the book with a chapter on the conflicts, which I think represent the true cause of our poverty. We became a nation when blacks and mulattoes put their strength together to fight Napoleon. Unfortunately, the preconditions of nationhood were not completely fulfilled at that time. I added a chapter on the continuous decline of our agriculture. I wrote about the elitism of our education system, our corruption and our dependency on foreign aid. I think that the planning ministry and the budget allocation should be adjusted. In conclusion, I tried to prove my starting hypothesis that: Haiti is in country locked in poverty.

The Indictment

Famous Haitian writer Louis Joseph Janvier used to refer to Haiti as a singular small country. One aspect of that singularity has been our survival in a hostile environment. Especially after a slave revolt vanquished the French, superpower of that time. The unique victory of slaves against masters in that hemisphere occurred in this island. The niggers had no choice. That was the best response in front of bad treatments they received from their oppressors. Abandoned by all, Haiti became a failed State. Under napoleon demand, the United States of America imposed an embargo against Haiti. Even Simon Bolivar could not help us. Haiti had to wait until Abraham Lincoln proclaimed the end of slavery to sit down on the table with other Nations of the Hemisphere. We paid to Paris $ 150.000.000 for our independence. That payment will put Haiti in bankruptcy forever. Our gross receipts could not pay for our expenses.

At the beginning of the 20th century, with the Monroe Doctrine in application, the Haitian nation became under the radar of the growing American imperialism. They helped us paying off the debt to France. However, American investors did nothing for Haiti because of our agricultural system of small-scale property. When they left the country, we became divided in two clans: the mulatrists and the noiristes. Since then, Haiti political

1

system has been revolving around these two trends. The political power managed by the noiristes and the economic power belonging to the mulatrists. After a period of prosperity relative under Dumarsais Estime and Paul Magloire, the country went into a dark period of political dictatorship and economic recession under the regime of Francois Duvalier. The international community increased his aid to Jean Claude Duvalier, and we had an economic boom that lasted until 1984. An internal conflict broke between the Duvalierists, the Jean Claudistes and the Benettistes, then the regime collapsed in February 1986. The reinstallment of Jean Bertrand Aristide to power in 1994 by Bill Clinton caused the international community to resume financial aid in Haiti. Unfortunately, the hole created by the three years embargo imposed on the military rulers could not be filled in. Furthermore, too happy for the return of their leader, the lavalassiens did not take time to comprehend fully some papers signed in Washington. When they refused to obey to the deal, Washington dropped the regime. To avoid the corrupt Haitian civil service, the aid was confided to many NGOs. Since then this trend keeps going on and some journalists called Haiti, an NGO Republic.

The earthquake of January 12, 2010 threatens the existence of Haiti as a nation. Some international observers talk about a UN protectorate. As Haitian, I think we must be ready to pay the price of our uniqueness in that hemisphere. We can save our country by adjusting it to the globalization. The State born from the most prosperous Caribbean colony has become the poorest nation of the hemisphere and yet I see no light at the end of the tunnel.

CHAPTER I

Everlasting political conflicts: the Haitian curse.

To maintain their dominance on the colony of Saint Domingue, the French established a rigid cast system in which contacts and relations among citizens of different colors were legally forbidden. The prosperity of that colony attires the greed of all super powers of that time. For two centuries, British, French, and Spanish fought to control the Island. They had to wait until the Ryswick treaty in 1697 to divide the island in two: the west part to the French and the east part to the Spanish. The French took all the steps to transform that colony into the most flourishing in their crown. Commercial exchanges between French and Saint Domingue attained 11 millions USD meanwhile all the British colonies put together had a total exchange of 5 millions USD with their metropolis. To commerce with Saint Domingue, French mobilized a float of 750 boats. The principal products exchanged were: sugar, coffee, cotton, cacao, and woods. The treatment of slaves in Saint Domingue has been particularly brutal, with whipping, mutilation and torture. The 1789 French revolution transmitted new ideas for a new social contract among citizens. Emotions raised by that ideological uprising penetrated all social classes and the fight for change will go on until the end.

Andre Rigaud and Toussaint Louverture failed to work out a common strategy to fight white domination. The latter won the battle and took the leadership for social change in the colony of Saint Domingue. Toussaint wanted to transform the colony in a free associated state with the metropolis. As a reformist, he wanted to go slowly with the changes in order to avoid any suspicion in the Napoleon entourage. Unfortunately, the colons did not understand him. Treated as the black Napoleon by his admirers, the genial slave of Breda became the uncontested leader of the colony and a smart defender of the mass of slaves. He did not last too long and Napoleon Bonaparte ordered his arrest, then he will die under the hard conditions of his imprisonment.

Jean Jacques Dessalines and Alexandre Petion persisted with the fight and marched ahead of the troops until the final victory. The clause of the alliance Petion/Dessalines, leaders from two antagonist races were never revealed. The emotion raised by Napoleon intimidation to reinstate slavery in the colony forced that pact. The links of that chain seemed strong enough to defeat the troops of General Rochambeau. In the name of the fight for liberty and equality, Haiti was created. However, before the foundation of that State, one can ask if the necessary steps bringing nationhood were realized.

Since the Ryswick treaty, French and Spain were sharing the island possession. The revolt took place in the western part of the island under French dominance. Blacks imported from Africa to work in Saint Domingue plantations and mulattoes or Affranchis born of White fathers and black mothers shared that island for two centuries.

On January 1, 1804, celebrants of the Gonaives arm square were from two ethnic groups: blacks and mulattoes. That difference of color will constitute the main problem preventing the unity of the country. The mulattoes tend to reject their African past. They held the legacy obtain from their fathers. The language used and written by mulattoes was French and their religion was Roman Catholicism. Meanwhile the mass of illiterate from slavery could speak only Creole and practiced voodoo as their religion. Family structures were also different: mulattoes married meanwhile blacks families were created by free union. There was never a social contract at the time of gestation of the Haitian state. Mulattoes and blacks advanced as if each group embarked in a different boat. Mulattoes, the social group most educated thought that they could survive without the mass of ignorant blacks. The Haitian State did not benefit of a leadership able to weld national unity. All along the 19th century, the Haitian elite progressively detached of the mass. Some scholars went very far to call a caste system the division between the elite and the masses. Historically, Haiti never moved in the direction of homogenization to end the sharpness of the cleavage, which persisted in the society.

The murder of Jean Jacques Dessalines at Pont Rouge on October 17, 1806 in a plot planned by the mulattoes demonstrated the hypocrisy that built the alliance created before the independence. I do not understand why historians never studied on the antagonist character of the two ethnic groups who founded the Haitian State. Only the desire to fight Bonaparte put together two radically opposed groups. Dessalines proved his warrior quality, but they did not give him time to demonstrate his administrative talent. His ascension at the head of the newly created State did not make him forget his slave origin. After he had salvaged them from the chains, he wanted a separation of the national economic pie. For he had to confront the mulattoes who wanted to monopolize the big properties abandoned by the escaping colons. His murder took place at Pont Rouge in the western department under Alexander Petion leadership. In addition, that place is geographically close to PetionVille where mulattoes regrouped around Petion.

JEAN JACQUES ACAU AND THE "PIQUETS"

The color question rejected.

Alexander Petion periodically distributed lands to his supporters. We could not find in our search if the distributions were racially motivated. However, we can affirm that he was dedicated to dismantle the big properties by distributing the one belonging to the State. Not everybody was satisfied. The top generals of the indigenous army were the principal beneficiaries. In 1843, under the government of Jean Pierre Boyer, a mulatto named Acau revolted. He took the leadership of a group of peasants without land to form an army baptized piquets because of the type of weapon they used. His slogan was wealthy blacks are mulattoes and poor mulattoes are blacks. The 1843 movement as called by historians was the proof that the blind distribution of land failed. That was a posthumous victory of Jean Jacques Dessalines called the first socialist Haitian. He wanted that the State held the land possession left by the French colons. After the harvest, peasants would have to pay taxes to collectors. Acau was right to protest against the mode of land distribution by Petion and Boyer, but it was too late. The failure of our agriculture can be traced from that time. Under the weight of heavy taxes imposed by Port au prince, peasants will apply a strategy, which consisted in the shifting of production highly taxed to production paying fewer rights.

LIBERAL AND NATIONAL

Failure of the first attempt to install democracy in Haiti.

After the recognition of our independence, the new State started trading with the World. Some Europeans countries finally accepted to have relations with the State issued from a slave rebellion. The US embargo against Haiti ended after Abraham Lincoln abolished slavery. Very fast, Haitians copying the American and European models organize themselves in political parties. I could not find any documents explaining why the liberal party was in majority populated by mulattoes meanwhile mostly black scholars controlled the national party. Ideological debates were very intense at that epoch. That was the time where Haiti had a chance to turn to democracy. Haitians organized themselves in political parties. The national and the liberal party occupied the political space of the country. The ideological question turned to a color debate. The national party with his slogan "Power to the majority" worked like what we called today a populist group. The name of Jean Jacques Dessalines banished for decades after his mutilation at Pont Rouge could reappeared in intellectual circles. The liberal party had as slogan that "Power belongs to the most educated". In that, time talking about the most educated referred to the mulattoes who had the opportunity to complete their studies in French. As a result, the management of the country was up to them. Under the presidency of Lysius Felicite Salomon elected with the flag of the national party, the ideological debate turned to violence. Wishing to obtain the power by any means, a group of leaders of the liberal party organized a military invasion. They confronted the national party who won the fight and reinforced the power of President Salomon. That democratic experience which could have strengthened our nation by reinforcing of our political institutions failed pitifully. Before the organization of election, Salomon was overthrown by an insurrection and fled into exile as his enemies of the liberal party did in the previous years.

JUILLET 1915: THE WHITE LAND IN BIZOTON

New development in the color question.

Revolutions and Coups continued to dominate the Haitian political spectrum until the end of the nineteen century. For example, when a citizen wanted to become president, he put together a group of individuals and armed them. The next step started with the descent through Port au Prince. Once the insurgent's army arrived close to the capital, to avoid his capture, the president has no other choice, than to run away with his bags full of cash taken from the public treasury. The newly installed president had to take control of the Customs office in order to manage the gross receipts. The positive point of that time was the payment of the debt that all government respected. For all the 19th century up to the beginning of the 20th, trying to seize the presidency constituted the objective of all Haitian politicians. In a two-year period, four presidents succeeded giving an average of one Chief of State every six months.

The mass killing of political prisoners inside the central jail of the country offered to the Americans the occasion to execute what they have looked for at least one decade: the invasion of Haiti. Culturally, Haiti represented a part of French in the Caribbean. From the official recognition of our independence in 1825, Paris and Port au Prince normalized their relations in all domains. Salomon married a French woman and the relations between the two countries attained their height during that tenure. Paris refinanced the debt and created the national Bank of Haiti.

Next to our attachment to France, other European powers were interested to Haiti and normalized relations with the Negro State. At the beginning of the twenty first century, merchants originated from Germany began installing in Haiti. The German started competing with American interests in the Caribbean. Let us remark that the Monroe doctrine claiming that the continent belongs to the Americans represented the main vector of the American diplomacy and Haiti stayed under the American radar.

The first German businesspersons who settled in Haiti married to Haitian women in order to avoid Haitian laws, which prohibited foreign possession of land. That strategy allowed them to conquer rapidly the heart of the Haitian elite who fraternized with them. In this way, they got ahead of the Yankee in commercial competition in Haiti. They established in almost all the Haitian provinces. Haitians were welcome when they travelled to Europe; meanwhile in USA they felt badly the racial segregation, way of life of the American society. Marriages between Haitian women and Germans created a generation of Haitian Germans who reinforced the link between the two countries. In 1912, the German government created a school in Haiti. According to officials, they intended to Germanize the children born here.

From 1914, Germans controlled 80% of the Haitian business sector. The assumed the management of the only Port au Prince Warf. Almost two thirds of Haitian exports were transported by German boats.

Very few American citizens were residing in Haiti and the cultural relations between the two nations were insignificant. The proximity of Haiti with the USA played no role in the commercial expansion of the two nations. The amount of American investments in Haiti by 1914 was $4 million USD compared to 220 million USD in Cuba and 800 millions USD in Mexico.

The plot to invade Haiti was planned by the State Department and the First National City Bank. Roger Farnham, PDG of City Bank who worked closely with Mr. Josephus Daniel, Secretary of the Navy, financed Haiti's political upheavals of 1914-1915. Their objectives were clear: find the ideal pretext to invade and occupy Haiti. As the cacos came close to Port au Prince, General Charles Oscar decided to empty the jail by organizing a massacre. Eyewitnesses reported they could see the blood of victims pouring until the doors of the prison through Center Street. Awaken by the chocking news of the blood bath, the populace invaded the streets and the president Vilbrun Guillaume Sam was lynched. In the afternoon of that sad Friday, 330 marines debarked in Bizoton, an area south of Port au Prince. The first Negro republic passed under the control of the executants of the Monroe doctrine.

THE OCCUPANTS, CHARLEMAGNE PERALTE AND THE REINSTATEMENT OF THE CORVEE.

In the night of their invasion, the occupants went under the fire of Caporal Pierre Sully in the South of Port au Prince. The nocturnal patrol of the Yankees had to walk in the middle of the road to avoid receiving in their faces the garbage coming from houses closed to the road. The situation aggravated for the inhabitants of Port au Prince who could not shop for their foods because parallel to the intervention an army cacos was marching down toward Port au Prince. Doctor Rosalvo Bobo was the instigator of that ultimate insurrection. The invaders ordered food directly from US in order to supply the hungry persons of the capital. That action taken by the invaders relieved a part of the population from starvation. Nevertheless, under the insistence of the secretary of State Josephus Daniels, food distributions stopped. In a letter written to President Wilson, he mentioned his apprehension: "" it is very dangerous to continue with food distribution because Haitians like Negros from the south of USA will give up plantations"

At the time of the US intervention, the national network road built by the French was obsolete and modern vehicles of the invaders could barely circulate throughout the cities. With the lack of funds for such public works, the Americans pulled out from the drawers an old law dated from 1864. According to that law, peasants had to work in road constructions to avoid paying taxes. The name of that ancient practice was corvee. That decision to reestablish that old method was resented as an insult by Haitian peasants. Let us mention that many of them owned their parcel to cultivate. That situation favored recruitment by Charlemagne Peralte and he built a guerilla army that became the symbol of the anti occupation. Furthermore, the massacres of peasants by American troops augmented the energy of Peralte men. In a short period, his army grew to attain 40.000 men. Unfortunately, the cacos of Peralte badly trained and equipped fought only with their heart. The Americans wiped them out and Charlemagne Peralte was crucified after his betrayal by an informant named Jean conze. Now after the sinking of the revolt, the occupants rebuilt a new-armed force to replace the old gendarmerie.

MULATRISME

Since the war of the South between Andre Rigaud and Toussaint Louverture, the roots of mulatrisme and noirisme were implanted. After the independence, the fight went on with the understudy politic where mulattoes installed a black President while they hold the true command of the power. Before the intervention, 11 black's Presidents had occupied the Palace. Rosalvo Bobo and Sudre Dartiguenave became finalists of a presidential election organized by admiral Caperton and the captain Beach. In front of the nationalism of Dr Bobo, the Americans preferred the Senate president Sudre Dartiguenave. This one, Mussolini admirer and of the fascism ideology did a lot of concessions to the invaders. He accepted to give up the control of our customs, of the Saint Nicholas mole, the national Bank, and to finish paying the money for the unfinished works of the railroad. Sudre Dartiguenave wanted the protection of the marines against the hostility of the Haitian mass. Then they named Louis Borno to succeed Dartiguenave for 4 years. Like his predecessor, he saw the occupation as a good thing for the country that will help improve some of the country problems. He collaborated closely to Russell, the American high commander and Cumberland the financial advisor who insulted him in many occasions. According to Hans Schmidt (p128), the Haitian President Louis Borno had to bend his head and tried to become Cumberland good friend because he held his paycheck to force him to more respects.

After the strike by Agronomist students and the trouble that followed, the Americans switched their strategy. They accepted the election of a nationalist mulatto personalized by Stenio Vincent. To the contrary, of his predecessors, the latter took side for the departure of the American troops. On August 15 1934, he proclaimed himself as the second liberator after Dessalines. He held the power until the election of his successor Elie Lescot. The latter was the representative of Haiti in Washington under the government of Stenio Vincent. Under his administration, only mulattoes could access to the high political functions.

The result of the first American occupation of Haiti until recently constituted a matter of debate among Haitian intellectuals. We think that many changes occurred in the management of public goods. Our isolation of the world ended and most European countries followed the US path. American businesspersons invested in tourism, sugar, and banana. The creation of a powerful army should assume political stability in the country. However, Americans had not abandoned racism, which is a way of life in their country. A movement called indigenous inspired by Jean Price Marc book" the uncle has spoken" developed in the Haitian black middle class. That period will determine the political future of the country.

THE JANUARY 1946 WIND

Before the American invasion and the election of Sudre Dartiguenave blacks and mulattoes president were elected alternatively. The Haitian politic scene was dominated by a concept called understudy, which allowed mulattoes to hold the real power while a black occupied the presidency. For the 19 years of the American occupation, only mulattoes occupied the presidency. Haitian scholars remain divided concerning the occupation result. For some members of the Haitian elite favorable to the occupation, the US could have helped us develop Haiti, but the long fight with the cacos prevented that. On the other side, that occupation has lifted a nationalist trend that will occupy the political spectrum after the departure of the troops. The Americans have tried everything to make the occupation a success. They built bridges, roads, and public offices. They reformed our civil service. They cleaned our public finance permitting Haiti to have a positive credit rate in the international markets. Do not forget that they are not used to a system in which government takes over the life of citizens. That is a capitalist model where private sector does businesses.

Among the four mulattoes that gained access to the power, Elie Lescot was the one who applied political segregation openly. Historian Roger Dorsainville in his book "walking backward" reports that after being hired for a position in the Lescot government, he had to abandon it because of the racist atmosphere of that regime. In addition, President Lescot chased severely leftist scholars in that country. Tired of that segregationist President, at the beginning of January 1946, schoolchildren and students took the streets asking Lescot departure. Some eyewitnesses of those events continue to talk or to write about the 1946 revolution. However, our search did not lead us to any trace of revolution. Dumarsais Estime enjoyed the dividends by becoming the president during a controversial second-degree election. I had the chance to read an essay published by Scholar Leslie Manigat in the chuduca notebook where he revealed the names of many actors of that event. I counted as many blacks as mulattoes plotting the uprising. Why some scholars speak about noirisme victory? Louis Dejoie, a mulatto elected senator of the western department was an authentic actor of January 1946. Dumarsais Estime married a mulatto woman. The coup of May 10 1950 propelled Army General Paul Magloire to the presidency. For years after, Haitian politicians will talk and write about the 1946 revolution. After analyzing many papers written about that event, we could not conclude that a revolution took place in Haiti in 1946. The nationalist and indigenous wake occasioned by the 19 years of American occupation kept going after their departure. Do not forget that all the Haitians President of the occupation period were mulattoes. Lescot intolerances pushed the newly promoted black middle class to fight for a better share of the national pie. They intended to substitute to the mulattoes in the civil service.

DUMARSAIS ESTIME:
THE DEMOCRATIC LEFT IN POWER IN HAITI

Even today, the name of Dumarsais continues to resonate through Haiti as the greatest President this country ever elected. This farmer's son rose through the ranks and became a prominent figure of the black bourgeoisie that has always coexisted with the traditional oligarchy. We cannot find it through the leaders of the strike that led to the fall of Lescot; however, he was at the forefront of the events of 1946. There was no revolution; it was only a week of nationalist and social explosion quickly taking in control by the traditional politicians. The resentment of many members of the black middle class against the colorism of the Lescot administration. was the basis of the uprising. The prompt intervention of the Army with the formation of a Junta of three members killed in the bud any attempt of a revolutionary movement. After seven months of negotiations and political maneuvering, Dumarsais Estime, the least popular candidate was elected to the presidency. The candidate of the Popular Socialist Party (PSP), Demosthenes Calixte, was defeated because it was an election in the second degree. The steamroller of Daniel Fignole could not do anything for Calixte during the vote in the House.

Dumarsais Estime and the mulattoes

Dumarsais Estime was a clever politician and he managed the issue of color and class, our main sources of conflict, with exceptional control. He called into his cabinet two members of the movement of workers and peasants: François Duvalier and Daniel Fignole. He kept the mulattoes in leadership positions and they remained in control of the economic machine because of their experiences in the business sector. The black middle class constituted the base of the revolt against Lescot in order to run after political positions instead of engaging in business. They have become a class in competition with the rich mulattoes. Despite its popularity and balanced politics, Dumarsais Estime could not manage to retain power. In addition, the new black middle class, which replaces the mulattoes in the public administration, have done nothing better than their predecessors. The moguls of the oligarchy were watching and at the right time, Estime was dethroned.

May 10, 1950: Coup d'état of the Army.

Despite the constitutional prohibition, Dumarsais Estime and his supporters wanted to organize an operation for re-election. The situation degenerated rapidly since many problems have arisen in terms of preventing re-election. The leftist opposition has facilitated the game for the right-wing oligarchy. A movement led by leftist socialists representing the claims of the student and unionized groups attacked the government. Estime fought them fiercely because they blamed their ultra-nationalism but also to satisfy the United States of America which as always is watching leftist infiltration in Latin America and the Caribbean. This agitation created the subjective conditions for a coup favoring the traditional oligarchy who wanted to take over the monopoly of power lost in 1946. Paul Magloire alias kanson Fe played a crucial role in the coup that brought to power Estime. He installed connections and informants in the back of the President and he knew that senators would prevent the attempt to retain power by Estime and his supporters. The awkward action of the president henchmen trying to intimidate the parliament by noisy demonstrations and social unrest maintained by the workers and peasants has been a pretext for the military to intervene not only to keep the peace in the streets but also to safeguard the constitution. The General Paul Magloire took power, the Catholic clergy welcomed him, and the U.S. Embassy saw in him the guarantee of public safety. A fraction of the middle class opportunist who nevertheless had supported Estime changed their coat for Paul Magloire.

Paul Magloire, a caudillo of the far right.

In his explanation of the seizure of power, General Paul Magloire emphasized the need to restore the social order, to permit the orderly development of the nation. Paul Magloire regime has marked the political life in Haiti with a dictatorship dominated by the army and by a black police chief called all-powerful Marcaisse Prosper. To maintain the color balance in the interior of the army, a group of young and ambitious mulattoes' officers dominated the army and occupied the command positions. Many political figures that had held the stage before 1946 appeared again. To support the regime they considered as a client government, the United States of America encouraged businesspersons and adventurers in quest of profits to invest in Haiti. The great favor that Washington accorded to Magloire could be read through some mainstream American Medias such as The New York Times and News Week. They did not hesitate to post the photo of the Haitian black General in their front page. Magloire regime has reached its peak during his official visit to Washington during which he met with President Dwight Eisenhower. The latter assured him of U.S. support in all areas on behalf of the visceral anti- communism view the two Presidents shared.

THE LONG DUVALIER'S PERIOD.

On September 1957 took place a presidential election in Haiti dominated once again by colorist passion. The two finalists represented the camps that were fighting to control the power since the creation of the Haitian State. According to some eyewitnesses, Louis Dejoie made a speech in Gonaives town where he said that if he won the election a mulatto should represent Haiti in Washington. That declaration made by candidate Dejoie threw a sector of the army to the Duvalier's camp. Grandson of former president Fabre Geffrard, he received a first class education in French. The slogan of his party "PAIN" reflected his economic program. Influenced by his formation of engineer agronomist, he wanted to modernize the Haitian agriculture. He told that only agriculture could save Haiti. In front of him, Francois Duvalier, Doctor in medicine representing that middle class issued of the American occupation. Militant of noirisme, he collaborated with the notorious Marxist Jacques Roumain. His party "UNITY" wanted to improve the life of the mass from the countryside. Duvalier won and the aftereffects of his tenure continue to influence Haitian political scene nowadays. Elected in ballots, he is going to transform his presidential regime for life and with the rights to elect his successor.

DUVALIER AND THE COLOR PROBLEM.

Migrated from the French colony of Martinique, Duval Duvalier settled in Carrefour, a quarter South of Port au Prince. It was there that Urutia Abraham gave birth to Francois Duvalier. Later, the family will move to Bel Air, a quarter in the center of Port au Prince where Duval worked as a judge. After graduation from the secondary cycle, the young Duvalier was admitted to the school of Medicine. He obtained his doctorate there, and then travelled to Michigan to accomplish some graduate studies. Back to Haiti, he worked as a professional doctor and became famous among the peasants for heading a campaign to cure an outbreak of a special foot disease. That short glance in the life of Duvalier shows that he climbed the social ladder on his personal efforts. Some observers want to stigmatize his tenure as an anti mulatto reign. They said that some mulatto's families were persecuted specially from members of the militia. In addition, following political trouble with Duvalier, some families were destroyed in Jeremie, Jacmel, cazal etc.

Nonetheless, in duvalierist circle we could find many mulattoes. For example, one of them the renowned Frederick Duvigaud became his first interior ministry. Testimonies of some mulattoes are favorable to Duvalier. They think at the beginning the regime of Francois Duvalier functioned as one of the most pragmatic

Haiti ever known. However, throughout years, unnerved by the harassment of his enemies, the gouvernement will transform in a killing machine. Inside the militia, the army, and secret services worked many mulattoes partisan of the regime. The traditional mulatto arrogance reinforced by the 19 years of the US occupation vanished and many of them fled into exile. In good opportunistic, Duvalier played sometimes the American game and sometimes the demagogy of noirisme. In both cases, mulattoes found themselves stuck in the middle. To face the regime of Fidel Castro installed in Cuba, Washington permitted to Duvalier to remain for life to power in order to protect capitalist interests in the Caraibes. Since the beginning of the 30s, Haiti was penetrated by the Marxist ideology. Many young mulattoes who studied in Europe came back to spread the ideology in the Island. Under the leadership of Jacques Roumain, a communist party was created in the country. After the premature death of Roumain, Marxism continued its way in Haiti. Duvalier contacted many friends in that circle, and then he used them to infiltrate the communist party. Another example of the Duvalier opportunism manifested in what historians called the Jacmel speech. To impress Washington in order to receive economic aid, Duvalier travelled to Jacmel a symbolic town of mulatrisme in Haiti. There he made a speech in which he threatened to turn the country in the communist sphere. He was right because the Americans will stop pushing him to organize election at the end of his term in 1963. He will never hold any election and the following year in 1964, he will proclaim himself as president for life until his death in April 1971.

Another aspect of the opportunistic character of Duvalier resided in his noirisme demagogic. The September 1957 election was a referendum on the color question in Haiti. Francois Duvalier and Louis Dejoie, two representatives of the middle class and the bourgeoisie in Haiti solicited from the electorate the presidency. The roots of those elections extended from the uprisings of 1946, in which the middle class revolted against the segrega-

tion of the public administration started at the time of the occupation, to attend its peak under the Lescot government. In that
context of race struggle, the majority of black intellectuals swung
in the Duvalier camp. An important faction of the army took side
for Duvalier. After the ejection followed by the exile of Daniel
Fignole, the black officers of the army turned for Duvalier. Most
of them will regret their choice because for fourteen years they
had to choose among the absolute submission, the jail for life, or
the exile forever.

In his program politic, candidate Duvalier promised to
improve life conditions of peasants from the countryside without
explaining how. We could not find in our search any economic
program elaborated by Duvalier government aiming at the
redemption of poor from the provinces. As soon as the end of
1957, the Hench men of Barbot transformed the nights of Port
au Prince in wakes for survival. DKW (made in Germany car)
crisscrossed the town at night with masked men who invaded
the houses to arrest citizens in their beds. In many cases, families will never see again their arrested members. All sectors were
hit: students, artists, businesspersons, intellectuals. It is in that
context that the exodus of the middle class and the small bourgeoisie started. From that time Port au Prince was invaded by a
mass of citizens from the countryside whom Duvalier referred
often in his dull speeches. The Duvalier's regime constituted the
symbol of administrative centralization in Haiti. Port au Prince
has become a Republic Capital and all decision must come from
the National Palace. In an article published by the daily paper
the novelist, Marc Bazin a renown economist mentioned that the
fall of the Haitian PIB started in the 60s after the wonder years of
Dumarsais Estime whom Duvalier had claimed the legacy.

The import-export sector under control of Arabic descents
was still the main center of activities in the country. Duvalier
never threatened them. They enriched them vastly and, their
accumulated profits were expatriated overseas. No investment
in the industry, agriculture or tourism was made which those

profits. In fact, the Francois Duvalier regime had not initiated any long-term economic development program. Many mulattos of the traditional bourgeoisie who found themselves in Dejoie camp in 1957, stayed away of the regime. Some of them fled the country in fear of political retaliation. After each attempt to overthrow his gouvernement, Duvalier organized blind arrests and executions. In the army and the civil service, the mulattos became a minority during Francois Duvalier tenure. In some cabinet ministry of Duvalier, no mulatto was named. For some observers, that was a tactical put in place by Duvalier to satisfy the noiristes in huge numbers in his government. As a Machiavelli disciple, they said that Duvalier knew how to divide his fans. For example, in 1967 in the conflict that opposed his two son-in-laws Max Dominique and Luc Albert Foucard, he decided in favor of the mulatto Foucard. Without the bravery of his daughter Marie Denise, Colonel Max Dominique, his son in law would have been the twentieth executed of June 18, 1967.

WHAT ABOUT DUVALIER'S?

At the height of its power, Francois Duvalier received a severe blame from "The international Commission of Jurists". In a paper, the jurists charged that Haiti had become the poorest country in Latin America because of the incompetence, inertia, and corruption of its government. Until then, no Haitian dictator ever used the power of force like Duvalier. On November 8, 1967 a commando, macoute robbed a Bank in broad day light. To flee, they used a small stolen bus-using siren like a police car. Everybody in Port au Prince knew that a macoute squad having Duvalier okay did the job. According to Al Burt and Bernard Diedrich :<< Duvalier has killed or driven his enemies or suspected enemies into exile with a ruthlessness perhaps surpassed only by the revolutionary Dessalines, who had at least the excuse of having felt the sting of the slave whip.>> Today, many Haitians in their seventies still talk passionately about the Duvalier epoch. They said at that time Haiti was a well-respected country and there are proud of him because he has defied the Americans who always interfere in Haitian affairs. Even Dominican dictator Raphael Leonidas Trujillo had to deal with Duvalier. Under Duvalier, the voodoo became a quasi-official religion. Hougans could enter the National Palace to bring advice to him at any time. Land conflicts in town like Gonaives, Saint Marc in the department of Artibonites were solved generally in favor of the hougans. Instead of solving the land conflicts, they had become worst. For having travelled a lot in the provinces, the little Doctor had a deep knowledge of peasants. He made them respond to him, to his cult of blackness, his love of brutality, and his medical degree. He brilliantly used the voodoo to enhance his stature, particularly among the lower class. Some duvalierists felt that papa doc suffered from a delusion that he was in constant contact with the voodoo gods and he thought he could travel into the spirits word. His strategy to place hougans as sheriff (chef section) in the rural areas made him appear as a high rank voodoo chief, a kind of super bocor. In 1964, Duvalier proclaimed himself as president for life and gravely ill, he asked his parliament to amend the constitution adding a paragraph allowing the nomination of his successor. He humiliated many of his close advisors and followers in January 1971, when he officially named his 19 years old son as the heir. As described by the journalist Jean Dominique in his famous editorials, Jean Claude Duvalier was like a prince surrounded by a group of regents under the order of his mother and sisters. After the passing of Francois Duvalier on April 22, 1971, Jean Claude was installed as president for life, the same title as his father. That was the end of the Duvalierism like it was practiced in the 1960s. It was the beginning of a new era: the Jean Claudism.

THE LEGACY OF FRANCOIS DUVALIER

During our two centuries of independent country, Francois Duvalier has been one of the presidents whose ideological impact lasted a so long period. Even after his death more than 40 years ago, Haitians continue to talk about Duvalier's in Haiti. While it is easy to define " Duvalier's " as a servant of the Duvalier regime, it becomes more difficult to explain to posterity the definition of Duvalierism as a doctrine or political ideology. In our national history, we talk about Dessalinien as those committed to the violent methods (cutting head, burned house) used by the Emperor to defeat the powerful army of Napoleon Bonaparte. In essence, Dessalinien means revolutionary. We talk about Louverturien in reference to those who continue to revere the diplomatic skill of the man from Breda to negotiate for the slaves. The famous historian Leslie Manigat writes about "breakthrough louverturien" to mean unexpected and spectacular changes of strategy and tactics of Toussaint Louverture.

Great characters and former senior officials of the Duvalier regime such as Clovis Desinor or Edouard Francisque never hesitated to proclaim their Duvalierist faith even in times of popular harassment. However, they never gave a clear definition of Duvalierism as a doctrine or ideology. François Duvalier has written books that explained his ascension to the Presidency of the Republic and its success against all opposition. Even between the lines, we could not detect if he was a rightist or leftist politician, but what seems clear is the cult of personality he maintained in his entourage about himself. It can be argued that he was a baron noiriste. Already in his writings with Lorimer Denis and other members of the School of griots, they never ceased to demand a greater share of the national pie for African descendants in this country. However, he worked closely with mulattos and many of them have contributed to his government. He considered himself as a leader of the third world, although he never left the National Palace. When he did so, it was in occasion of his rare visits in the provinces. An old intellectual from the Diaspora with whom I addressed the topic claimed that Duvalier had realized a social revolution in Haiti. As proof, he referred to the exclusive clubs and circles that some people could not access before Duvalier's rise to power. He reminded me that the Medical School, Military Academy and some diplomatic posts were once the preserve of mulattos. I replied that increasing enrollment in these institutions would have solved the problem because the mulattos in Haiti have always been a minority.

To close this parenthesis on Duvalier who remained an immortal for his supporters, meanwhile for his opponents he represents everything that is bad in this country, I will add a personal note by saying that Francois Duvalier was given an opportunity to retain the power; he seized the occasion to impose his creed, his dreams and achieved all his personal instincts.

JEAN CLAUDE DUVALIER: AFTER US, THAT US AGAIN.

Named by his father to his succession, Jean Claude Duvalier announced that he was going to win the economic revolution after his father had achieved the political revolution. The price of coffee had increased in the international market, the arrival of an important quantity of subcontract industries in Haiti, the country went over a long period of economic growth. The old color question seemed to be relegated to the past. In fact, Baby Doc counted in his periodic cabinet reshuffle some mulattos. During the celebration of the wedding between Jean Claude Duvalier and Michelle Bennet, the celebrant Bishop Francois Ligonde announced "the reconciliation of the two elites ". It was his way to recognize that under the Francois Duvalier regime, some mulattos were persecuted. A part of those elite returned in the country and put their entrepreneurial ability to serve Haiti. That trend was the start of the period of industrial subcontracting in Haiti that grew until the mid 80s. At the example of the countries named<< Asian tigers>>, Haiti offered to the multinational to exploit his low pay workers. At the end of the 70s, Haiti became the favorite place of investors in the subcontracting industry in the Caribbean. In the circle of the JeanClaudism, it was the triumph. Certain ministers as the famous Roger Lafontant compared Haiti to the Caribbean Taiwan. On the other side, a group of the bourgeoisie invested in the agro industry. That period remained of the most prosperous in the economic history of Haiti. The wedding of Jean Claude Duvalier and Michelle Bennett allowed mulattos to regain their political power in Haiti.

THE BENETTISME.

Before the wedding of Michelle with Jean Claude Duvalier, Ernest Bennett was a regular businessperson. They said he made a little profit in the export-import, especially in coffee in Cacao. Immediately after occupying the National Palace to live with the president for life, the fortune of the Bennett family changed. Michelle Bennett or the woman with big glasses (nickname given to the first lady by the mass) became omnipresent in everything. She named or revoked cabinet ministry when she wanted. She made transfers inside the army when she wanted. She was never easy for the macoutes who lashed her father in the 60s at the height of duvalierist repression. She became rich in a very short period. The transfer to her foreign accounts was executed in broad day light by the central Bank of Haiti (BRH). A powerful Colonel, military advisor of Jean Claude monitored the transfers. His fidelity had not prevented the first lady to fire him from the army because he knew too much about her businesses at the Central Bank. (Let us remind for history that surprised by that decision of the first lady, the powerful Roger Lafontant visited the revoked Colonel. Once in the living room the colonel bent on his knew to implore pity from Roger Lafontant). Michelle travelled often to New York to do shopping because she could not find in Haiti the type of clothing to wear in the specially refrigerated room placed in the National Palace. In spite of her vulgarity and her love of dirty words, she maintained a positive image of the public opinion. With a propaganda machine directed by the State owned television (TNH), her popularity went increasing.

Another branch of the Benettisme functioned under the command of her brothers. Those people meddled in all kinds of smuggling. The Bennett did not hesitate on any means to make money. Ernest Bennett refused categorically to pay Custom rights on his importations and verbally threatened employees if they did not obey. In all the ministers with a phone call of Bennett, any decision was executed within hours. There was no anti mulatto feeling in the country. The rising of coffee price and the openings added by the subcontracting industries of the industrial park permitted the Haitian economy to grow at a rate of 5%. That was the triumph for Jean Claude Duvalier who abandoned the repressive method of his father. As he repeated in his speech, he wanted to win the economic revolution after the political success of his father. The reconciliation of the two elites hoped by Mgr Ligonde did not occur in the corridors of the National Palace. The frequent skirmishes between Michelle Bennett and Simone Duvalier ruined the family atmosphere inside the Palace. The tension was so high that Simone had to move out from the Palace to live somewhere else. In addition, in a ceremony organized at the single branch parliament, Michelle was named first lady meanwhile Simone was proclaimed Guardian of the revolution. That conflict started inside the presidential family echoed through the political class. The old guard duvalierist had no other choice to accept the remoteness of Michelle Bennett. In the meantime, under the weight of too unbudgeted expenses, the budget deficit aggravated because they were so many people to satisfy. Already in 1981, the international monetary fund's (IMF) forced the government to place Marc Bazin at the Finance Ministry. He had for mission the cleaning of Haitian public finances. All the non-fiscal accounts which issued checks of the executives of the regime were placed in order by the Bazin administration. Mr. Clean as nicknamed by the international Medias had to help Jean Claude Duvalier put order in the house to save the regime. However, the old guard duvalierist held on and Mr. Clean was fired. His departure was celebrated with many parties organized inside the public administration. A special ceremony was organized in the diplomatic room of the Airport by some macoutes and champagne was drunken to celebrate the departure of that "kamoquin" who stopped too may check zombies. Unfortunately, for them, they chased a savior, after Bazin departure the regime will push deeply into an economic crisis. In April 1984, broke the hunger uprisings of Gonaives. Crying "down to poverty", people from Raboteau took the streets. Stones received the ministers sent to reinstate order and the glasses of the luxury cars were destroyed. Back in Port au Prince, one of them was fired for telling the truth to the president for life.

A STRANGE INCIDENT.

In a party organized at Kings Club located at Delmas, a banal incident occurred between two participants. In the fight the club owner, known as Baptiste intervened to restore the calm. However, a few shots were fired and one individual fall dead. He was identified as a henchman of Roger Lafontant. The shooter, Batiste a mulatto was a protégé of Theodore Achille also a mulatto in the inner circle of the first lady. Things turned to the worst and Theodore Achille was sent out of the cabinet ministry. Some observers saw the hands of Roger Lafontant in the cabinet ministry reshuffle confirmed by the fact that he went in the studio of the national television to read the announcement. The incident became a political event classified under the problem black-mulatto. However the Duvalier's boat was sinking. Two months after the king's club incident, the redoubtable Roger Lafontant was put under house arrest, and then exiled from the country. This time observers noted that the first lady who became very suspicious of Roger Lafontant took that decision. However, many persons in the inner circle of the regime signaled that that failure of the July 29 referendum to prove the popularity of the regime was the true cause of Roger Lafontant dismissal. He became so popular in the regime that the president for life had to spy his move in the National Palace. The duvalierist boat continued to sink slowly day after day. The budget deficit widened because too many people were on the payroll. The Haitian army watched the unfolding events closely and at the exact time plotted the fall of Duvalier with local politicians.

THE HAITIAN ARMY TOOK THE SUCCESSION.

To avoid a blood bath in the country, and to enter prestigiously in history, I have decided to transfer the power to the Haitian armed forces. That was the essential of the last message of Jean Claude Duvalier as president of Haiti. The incidents happened in Gonaives in the month of November, the anti governmental manifestation in a street closed to the National Palace in December after a concert were the two main subjects of political conversation at New Year's Eve. The year 1986 started with the traditional message of the president in which no indices signaled the imminent fall of the regime. Certainly, in the circle of opponents, they knew something was about to happen. Informed by their agents inside the country about the maturity of the plot against the regime, the state department through Larry Speaks announced in the night of January 30 the departure to exile of Jean Claude Duvalier. That announcement was a test to prove to Jean Claude Duvalier his unpopularity in Haiti and in the Diaspora. In the foreign countries with high concentration of Haitian, the people took the streets to celebrate. In Port au Prince the town of my origin, I saw for the first time a crowd chanting their happiness because of the Duvalier departure. However, early in the morning trucks filled with macoutes stopped all the manifestation of joy. Many people were arrested and beatings occurred in the middle of the street. We have to mention that the Captain Paul Casimir acted in an unusual way by talking quietly to the demonstrators inviting them to go home. By acting that way, he avoided a direct confrontation between the macoutes and the population out in huge number to celebrate the news of Jean Claude departure. Around 10 am, wearing plain clothe, the president for life toured the streets of Port au prince behind the wheel of a Range Rover. Questioned by a journalist, he declared the monkey tail has not broken yet. In the commercial area, activities resumed and the day ended peacefully. During the night, patrols of the army and the militia travelled through the streets. On Monday morning, life started again and nobody was talking about the false announced departure of the president. However, opponents to the gouvernement knew that something had to happen very soon. In that circle, nobody slept with both eyes closed. A rumor spread in the low quarters of the capital that names of persons were being placed on a list and that repression and arrests will begin soon. People were guessing in anxiety about their fate when at the dawn of Friday January 7, 1986, an incredible image stayed fix on the TV screen: the presidential couple was driving a luxury BMW escorted by two dressed army members sitting in the back sit. The Duvalier epic was over in Haiti.

In early morning, that was the turn of General Henry Namphy to pronounce a speech to introduce the National council of gouvernement as the successor of Jean Claude Duvalier. That 51-year-old mulatto was the head of the council. Few Haitians knew him before that because his name was not associated to the duvalierist repressions. Politically, nobody could classify him that general who survived the terrible purges of Francois Duvalier in the army. The black/mulatto problem had not splash up in the political arena, at least officially.

THE AMBIANCE DEMOCRATIC OF HENRY NAMPHY.

Among the five members of the National council taking command on February 7, 1986, Henry Namphy was the lesser known. Graduated from military academy as a lieutenant in 1956, he became the army top commander two years before the collapse of Duvalier. In fact, people who knew about the plot to outset Duvalier affirmed that General Namphy was an insider of the drama. He had to reshuffle the council because of political protest against Prosper Avril and Alix Cineas. He stayed in control of the council in spite of the upheavals provoked by the resignation of Gerard Gourgues nicknamed the wise guy of the council. He governed in a style that he baptized as ambiance democratic. Heavy drinker according to his inner circle, he continued his habit even when he became the head of the National Council of Government. The political of economic liberalization tried by Leslie Delatour resulted in a spectacular fall of price of some basic consumption products: milk, poultry, etc. In the short term Henry Namphy had benefited politically of that tricky economic policy. A new constitution was adopted only after the assembly members introduced an article excluding the duvalierist from the political arena for a minimum of ten years. For some unexplained reasons, the democratic sector wanted the dismissal of Colonel Regala (a black) meanwhile his associate, Henry Namphy (mulatto) enjoyed a good image through the Medias. During the election of November 1987, Namphy proved that he could change his good person image according to the circumstances. Dozens of electors were shot only because they aligned to vote. The members of the provisional electoral council took refuge in foreign embassies. Two months after that, on January 17, 1988 a funny election was organized among the least popular candidates of the last election and Leslie Manigat was picked as President of the Republic. The most popular candidates became members of an alliance to boycott the masquerade. During the swearing ceremony of the elected President, the laughs of General Namphy and Regala predicted that something burlesque was about to happen. After only four months of tenure, Leslie Manigat was trapped in a conflict opposing General Namphy and Jean Claude Paul. The general imitated a fake signature of the president to fire the colonel. After receiving the letter, the colonel went furious in the office of the President that he contributed to the election to know about this sudden firing. The President denied any responsibility and signaled to the powerful colonel that the signature was false. For unexplained reasons, Leslie Manigat decided to reform the army. Henry Namphy was dismissed from his post of command and placed under house arrest. Prosper Avril who was also transferred from the presidential guard rang the bell of unity inside the army. Only 72 hours after the transfer of rank in the army, armored vehicles drove to the Villa Moira for uninstalling Leslie Manigat as president. During the same night, army tanks went to Lilavois in order to reinstate General Henry Namphy as President for the second time and his new tenure will last only for three months. On September 17, 1988, a group of soldiers and officers took side against general Namphy. The rebellion was under the leadership of Patrick Bauchard, an army sergeant of the presidential guard. The General was handcuffed with dirty rope, shake, and put in an army tank. Then the convoy drove to the international Airport, placed the General in a small plane to be expulsed to Santo Domingo. The soldiers installed General Prosper Avril as the new president. Let us remind for history that faking to accompany his children to the USA for the new school year; General Avril realized an express visit in Washington, a day after the massacre of Sunday September 11, 1988 perpetrated in the Salesiens Church by Henchmen wearing red pieces of clothes in their arms.

THE ELECTION OF 1990.

After the massacre of the Vaillant Street on November 29 1987 orchestrated against parishioners, the democratic sector grouping all the leftist parties reorganized them. During that time, the division inside the military hierarchy became more pronounced. The successive coups proved that things were fainting inside the army. The prestige of the military institution was greatly affected. Haitians military had not realized that a trend of democracy was crossing Latin America. In addition, they found themselves on the opposite side of Washington global strategy in the region. The general Prosper Avril benefited of a coup realized by the army based. However, information from well-informed sources revealed that the general made a secret tour of Washington, hours before the coup. His commanders inside the big agency gave him order to drop Namphy. What is the difference between Avril and Namphy? The situation of the country had not changed. The insecurity extended in the country and each night strangers penetrated inside the homes to kill innocent citizens. Washington did not take any initiative to help the military regime. The traffic of drugs became a way of life of some members of the army to gain fortune. Profiting of that opportunity, drug lords in Latin America invaded Haiti and within a short period, the country was transformed as a taking off point of drugs designated to the immense US market. The general Prosper Avril attempted to organize a political forum, but a vast majority of the opposition sabotaged the initiative. The reaction of the general was immediate. Three of the main activists of the democratic sector were arrested: Evans Paul (KID), Jean Auguste Mesieux (CATH), and Patrick Bauchard (one of the coup organizers putting Avril to power). They were tortured and presented to the Haitian nation in a film that chocked the country. The general lost his credibility before the Haitian political class and the society as a whole. At that moment a new American ambassador, Alvin Adams was leading the American diplomacy in Haiti. Nicknamed Bourik Charge, because in a fluent Creole he could say an Haitian proverb" bourik chage pa kampe "(Charged Dunkey do not have time to waste). He entered the Haitian political arena as one the most popular diplomats ever to reside in that country. Feeling secured by his presence, the Haitian opponents to the military organized the chase of Prosper Avril from the power. In fact, he became more powerful after the failure of a coup attempted to overthrow him by a sector duvalierist of the army. After his surprised arrest in the night of March 31, 1989, he was liberated by a group of soldiers under the leadership of Sergeant Joseph Hebreux co President of the gouvernement with Prosper Avril. The rebels were jailed and expulsed from the country. Arrived in USA, they were put in jail back because the head of the big agency in Haiti had not authorized the coup. He won that round of the fight, but in front of Bouric charge, things were not so easy.

Students of the faculty mobilized and days of strike were organized by the sector syndical. The bourik put all its force in the battle and Prosper Avril gave up the fight. For the first time, a woman managed the country: Herta P Trouillot. Her mission was to organize the election as soon as possible.

In the month of July 1990, a surprised guess, Roger Lafontant, former macoute chief and interior ministry until September 1985 debarked in the country. His mission was to reorganize the duvalierist under a single command.

The left used the same procedure of 1987 by forming a united front with Victor Benoit as their candidate succeeding Gerard Gourgues the potential winner of the 1987 election turned ugly. The duvalierist answered by organizing a congress at Vertaillis where Roger Lafontant was selected as their candidate. A new electoral council was put in place and curiously, the same members exiled in 1987 took back their function in the electoral agency.

Bourik chage maintained good relations with all political sectors in Haiti. In a talk with the former priest whose church was burned down by Henry Namphy and Frank Romain henchmen, questioned him about his silence in the electoral process going on. In the circle closed to the priest, that question was assimilated to an invitation to the marching electoral train. In an antidemocratic pirouette, the left organized a new party labeled national front for democratic change (FNCD) and during a meeting; they got rid of Victor Benoit in favor of Aristide. Surprised by that move, Professor Victor Benoit gave up without a fight by shouting only the adventurist aspect of that decision. Persons well informed on the left whispered that the fear of Roger Lafontant provoked that change. Marc Bazin reputed the men of Washington was the favorite of the polls. The announcement of Aristide candidacy produced a choc amid the population, and public opinion gave him ahead of the poll. A bomb placed by an expert hand during a campaign visit to Kenscoff of the candidate returned the public opinion in his favor. The election took place on December 16, 1990 and Jean Bertrand Aristide was elected president of Haiti. His victory was magnificent.

They were preparing for the installation of the newly elected President on February 7, 1986 and the country was about to take a turn. Suddenly bitten by a crazy mosquito, Roger Lafontant with the complicity of some militaries embarked in two tanks of the army, went into the National Palace to proclaim in a televised message that he was the new President. It was January 6, 1990, day of the Kings according to the Catholic calendar, celebrated in Haiti as a mystic day. They said he made a phone call to Bourik charge to inform him of his initiative. He addressed him in his terms: Mr. Ambassador, I am in control of the Palace to assume the comeback of the duvalierism to power. Bourik chage answered him; in a few minutes, we are going to see that. After the televised message of President Lafontant, the people of Port au Prince took the streets. In a move comparable to an army, they circled the National Palace and Roger Lafontant was made prisoner. The former interior ministry had just danced his last rokn'roll. On the aftermath of the September 30, 1991 coup, he will be killed with a single shot by an invisible hand. The comedy played by the group of rebellious led by Roger Lafontant had placed a hole in the ball of democracy launched at high speed. It will be patched very rapidly.

In a festive morning on February 7, 1991, Jean Bertrand Aristide sworn in as the new President of Haiti. As a good disciple of Sylvain Salnave or Daniel Fignole, Aristide entered the National Palace as a populist. Many poor people took part to the ceremony. Nobody knows how many representatives of the economic elite of the country were invited. During the celebration Bayard Vincent, Port au Prince's Attorney general, threw a mandate at the former President Herta Trouillot. They said Aristide did not want her to flee the country before the end of the ceremony. In that case, why they did not put her on interdiction to leave the country at the Airport? In the National Palace during the inaugural speech, Titid acted again, he publicly insulted the colonels responsible of his security and fired them from the army and invited the world to be witness of the decision. He invited an army of poor to come dining with him in the National Palace. Moreover, he continued with the threats directed to Mr. X: << stone living in fresh water will know the same pain as stone in the sun >>.

He chose Rene Preval as his prime minister to manage the government. Comrades of the front who picked him to become their candidate were ignored. One former president from Venezuela and a high rank diplomat from the USA advised the formation of a government opened to all sector, but the former priest refused arguing that he has obtained 67% of the vote. That was in that atmosphere that the regime named Lavalas began leading the country. Their electorate was in the people of the shantytowns surrounding Port au Prince and some opportunists of the bourgeoisie. He threatened openly anyone who had a job in the civil service or every person who showed a social success. Since he was not used to the business circle, the former priest had not realized that his regime was being boycotted by the international source of financing. Even the non-profits organizations were not bumping into each other at Port au Prince. No plan of economic growth was put in place by the gouvernement. Rumors of coup filled the atmosphere. In the circle closed to the duvalierist and the military, several persons were arrested. The judgment of Roger Lafontant provided a good mean of diversion to the population. All the data were reunited for a populist government condemned to fail on its own.

THE SEPTEMBER 30, 1991 COUP.

It was Sunday September 29, 1991 and the capital of Haiti, Port au Prince, woke up with the same proverbial unattractiveness. Suddenly, sporadic shooting and heavy gunfire from automatic rifles were heard around the military academy of Frères. Noises of the shooting lasted all day and no official from the government took the stand to explain the population what was going on. Like what happened a few months earlier during the failed coup of Roger Lafontant, people invaded the streets in support of the government. However, that time the reception was different. Eyewitnesses and victims remembered seeing vehicles trucks shooting straight to the people in the streets of Port au Prince. We could not find the transcript of the speech made by Raul Cedras to explain the motive of that bloody coup. Months before, the army thwarted a previous coup attempt after the mass gathered in the streets to defend the President they have voted on December 16, 1990. Personal misunderstandings among members of the armed forces with the newly elected government were not sufficient to overthrow a government so popular. In fact, that is the reason explaining the violence used by the militaries to force people out of the streets. That coup had just confirmed the unpreparedness of the army to put the country toward the road of democracy confided to them five years ago.

Tim Weiner, a journalist American in his book << Legacy of ashes >> comments the decision of former president Bill Clinton to return Jean Bertrand Aristide to power in October 1994. He wrote the following: << The images of dragged dead soldiers through Mogadiscio streets were new in the public mind. Clinton wanted to reinstate the priest to power although he was told that Aristide was a leftist. He wished to do justice to the Haitians mass because Aristide represented the symbol of legitimacy. In order to do that, they had to chase the military junta who overthrown Aristide from power. Most leaders of the junta found themselves on the payroll list of the CIA for years spying for clandestine operations. That reality deceived the White house surprisingly. The revelation that the CIA created an intelligence service in Haiti whose military chiefs was distributing Colombian cocaine in Haiti, killing their political enemies, and protecting their power in Haiti. The CIA was placed in the difficult position to chase its own agents, which prorogued a conflict between the agency and Bill Clinton. Clinton rejected the assessment that Aristide was not an example of virtues. Woolsey described the conflict as purely ideological. The president and his aides' desesperately wanted that the CIA showed Aristide as that next Haitian Thomas Jefferson. We from the CIA refused and showed Aristide both faces. We were not popular because of that, Woolsey was right. The white house was not convinced by the analysis of Aristide weaknesses presented by their agency. In addition, they found the attitude of the rebellious very chocking. >>

That paragraph related by Tim Weiner in his book gives some clues and can help us understand the complexity of the September 30, 1991 coup d'état. Why some organizations defended so vehemently the putchists? For many observers with whom I share the opinions, that coup has represented a brutal stop to the political transition started five years earlier. General Raul Cedras and President Jean Bertrand Aristide within the same age group in spite of their difference of origin could have assumed the reconstruction politic and economic of the country. The former Bishop of Port au Prince Francois Ligonde had spoken about the reconciliation of the two elites in May 1981 while celebrating the wedding of Jean Claude Duvalier and Michelle Bennet. Surely, he wanted to stigmatize the noiristes origin of Jean Claude Duvalier and the mulatriste descent of Michele Bennett. The nomination of Raul Cedras as the commander of the army received a round of applauds amid the political class. A black sat down in the presidency while a mulatto led the army. One could have hope that this new reconciliation of class could have more impact because of the political conjuncture in the country. Raul Cedras is a mulatto of the small bourgeoisie and his parents have been long time allied to the Duvalier regime. His brother Didier occupied executive positions in the Jean Claude Duvalier administration. In fact, all his promotion at the military Academy was friends of Jean Claude Duvalier. Jean Bertrand Aristide is a black face from working class family. They said his families were poor and from the South of the country. Orphan very early in his life, he grew up under the protection of Salesiens Brothers and he became a priest of that order. After leaving Haiti to study abroad, he came back at the beginning of the 80s to spread the liberation theology in Haiti. By that same token, he has occupied the center of opposition to the Duvalier regime. I remember that some friends of mine used to invite me to listen to his sermons on Sundays at Saint Jean Bosco. Consequently, in 1991, Haiti could finally enjoy the charisma of those two leaders to start a reconciliation process, which would have cleared the way for an economic take off hoped for years.

However, as always in that country, the invisible hand of division acted covertly. The writing of that American journalist mentioned above in that chapter allows us to understand the origin of our misfortune and our political division. We are a poor country and our national budget is in deficit for years. The journalist writes that the executants of the 1991 coup were on the agency payroll for years and they were paid to answer to obey the big agency. That let us that question why the need to overthrow of a legal government after only seven months? I think that the coup allowed Aristide to win political dividends that he would not have obtained after five years of tenure. I was convinced that Aristide had not the leadership to operate the necessary changes in the country. An organized opposition could beat his party in the next election of 1996. Like that occurs here in USA, Santo Domingo and everywhere in Latin America and the Caribbean. During the riots in Santo Domingo in 1980, they did not organize a coup against the president of the Dominican Republic. Some former comrades of Raul Cedras mentioned that he is a mulatrist, a kind of supremacist ideology practiced by many mulattos since

Andre Rigaud. They said that Aristide is an autocrat and populist. Knowing the difference between those two leaders, the enemies of the Haitian nations paid the General to derail the democratic process in the country. Furthermore, an economic embargo was imposed in the country for three years in order to put pressure on the rebellious. The GDP of the country fall down between 25 and 30%. Some businesspersons were completely ruined. Haiti has become the center of Drugs in the Caribbean.

BILL CLINTON AND THE RETURN OF CONSTITUTIONAL ORDER IN HAITI.

According to the professor Noam Chomsky, candidate Bill Clinton favored the coup in Haiti against the priest thought to be a leftist in Washington. However, once in the command, the new president switched direction and now wanted the return to constitutional order. General Raul Cedras changed puppets by replacing Jean Jacques Honorat with Marc Bazin. Let us signal that the Economist- agronomist Jean Jacques Honorat lost his respect in that operation. We have to mention the opportunistic character of some Haitian scholars. Why activists fighting for changes and the economic development of the country take part at such slap to the national sovereignty? In fact, Jean Jacques Honorat will be completely out of mind. Marc Bazin, nicknamed the looser by his foreign bosses has spent all his political career serving contradictory governments. The militaries were abandoned by all the opportunistic who realize that Bill Clinton was not playing about Aristide come back. The economic embargo on Haiti was strengthening which put the country and the military rulers on their knee. In spite of all that pressure, knowing the support of the big agency they resisted the Clinton administration. On October 30, 1993, they defied the marines by preventing a warship to accost the Warf of Port au Prince. It was still early. Now, in the middle of his term and pushing his agenda, Bill Clinton wanted to stop with that farce. This time the orders are strict and the invasion is impeding. Informed by insiders on the high probability of an American invasion, the rebellious rushed to exile under boos of the people. Early in the morning of that Saturday October 15, 1994, Jean Bertrand Aristide was flown back to Haiti. People filled the streets of Port au Prince. Manifestations of joy were everywhere and the Haitian mass proved once again their naiveté. Many were killed in ambush by snipers or by heavy trucks driving straight into the crowd. It was the honeymoon between Aristide and the Clinton administration. In his speech, Aristide never mentioned the reasons and the hidden conditions of his return.

REVENGE TIME: DISMISSAL OF THE ARMY.

In December of 1994, two months after President Clinton decided to send the marines reestablish political order in Haiti, Jim Wolsey resigned from the CIA. He lost the fight against President Bill Clinton. His employees and agents of the military junta in Port au Prince were chased in order to allow the Haitians to enjoy their constitutional rights.

After the honeymoon of the first days, Aristide committed a mistake when he decided to disband the army during the year 1995. At first look, that was a pure revenge against his enemies. Once again, Aristide proved the weakness of his leadership. He is a good activist, but his management ability is not reflected in his decisions. The lack of democratic tradition in Haiti constitutes a living reality. The Americans created that version of Haitian army during the occupation of 1915-1934. It replaced the old weak Haitian Guards that cacos and Piquets attacked when they desired a change of President. Recruited in the civil society, almost all social classes melted in that army. After the occupant's departure, the Haitian army became an important actor on the social and political spectrum of the country. They represented a kind of warranty for social peace in a country so poor like Haiti. Humiliated by Duvalier (father and son), the army occupied the front scene of the country after the Fevrier 1986 events. Unfortunately, none of the General who occupied the power could find a way to maintain the professionalism of the institution. The army functioned as a machine of corruption and brigandage. All the Haitian political class knew that some member of the army were involved in cases of thefts and drugs trafficking. A fraction of the army realized the bloody coup of September 1991 and occupied illegally the power for three years. In spite of all those reasons against them, Aristide decision to disband them was not justified. An old adage states that nature has horror of emptiness. Aristide and his advisors did not take into account that saying. In addition, for the misfortune of the country, the following years represent the worst of Haiti as a nation. Maintaining social order has become a disaster for our leaders. The 1987 constitution on behalf of which Aristide returned as president makes an important place to the army. It is hard to understand that a constitutional president who has decided to banish an institution legally recognized by the same chart.

Ten years later, Jean Bertrand Aristide will obtain the reward of his lack of vision. His incomprehension of Haitian history will cost him his presidency. Armed and financed by hidden forces willing only to destabilize Haiti, groups of former soldiers invade Haiti in January 2004. Aristide could not count with the help of an army to fight them. The << chimeres >> a paramilitary group organized to threat his opponents were not trained for such mission. Aristide himself did not trust the police force he created; as a result he needed to pay a foreign company for his personal security. It was almost too late to correct the situation: in less than ten years, Haiti found itself again under occupation.

Since the founding of that nation 200 hundred years ago, the presidency has always occupied the center of political power. We do not have tradition of democratically elected President. The formation of coalition was very difficult and the election of a President was complicated. Most of the time personal alliances took place during election time. Before the American occupation of 1915, a Coup d'état represented the surest way to become President of Haiti. In the North (cacos) and in the South (Piquets), kind of gangs armed invaded Port au Prince whenever they wanted to overthrow a President. After the military success, the chief of the insurgency took over the Palace and proclaimed himself the new head of State. Nowadays, in spite of organized elections copied on the Western models, the relationship between the presidency, the Prime Minister, and the Parliament s still represent a source of conflict. Political parties are very weak. They are a band of unorganized clique which are united only during election time or when a plot is working out against the sitting President. In December 16, 1990, Jean Bertrand Aristide was elected President under the FNCD logo, an alliance built days before the scrutiny. The next day, December 17, he broke the alliance officially. He gave his co members, Turnep Delpe and Yvens Paul the following rationale: I had to use only your official hat. After his return from exile, the party OPl (platform organization of Lavalas) won the absolute majority in the parliament. That party also elected Aristide former Prime Minister Preval as President during the election of 1995. A few months later, Aristide distanced himself from the OPL by creating a new organization labeled "fami Lavalas". He systematically prevented Preval, his ex twin in politics to lead the country. Using the pretext to stop the application of the neoclassical policy in the country, his clique organized a lot of protest throughout the country that sometimes resulted in material damages. Prime minister, Rony Smart has to resign. In addition, a conflict broke inside the parliament and the OPL party lost many of its allies. Rene Preval led the country almost without a Prime Minister with a majority in the parliament during half of his term. Before such deficiency in the governance, what results can we expect in other sectors of the country, principally in the agonizing economy?

GUY PHILIPPE INVASION AND ARISTIDE KIDNAPPING.

The parallel government of Gerard Gourgues and Gerard Pierre Charles formed at the same time that Aristide was swearing on February 7, 2001 could not paralyze the government. Therefore, the group changed the strategy. A large alliance among the opposing groups took the name of convergence or the group of 184. After an attempt to kill Aristide in the National Palace on December 16, 2001, his partisans reacted violently and opposition leaders went into hiding. It was not a surprise. In the long account of our eternal misunderstandings, the readers will remark that each time, there is like an invisible hand plotting the course of events in that poverty ravaged country. Since that attempt of assassination, the possibility of dialogue became thinner and the chance of a political uprisings were inevitable. A well-informed source told us that while the political battle was going on, a former high ranked officer of the disbanded army travelled to Santo Domingo to meet Guy Philippe. He was an ex- police commissary in the national police, fired for being involved in drug trafficking.

The Aristide administration gave them a golden occasion to pass to the offensive. In fact, after the murder of an Aristide henchmen in Gonaives (Amiot Metayer) panicked the other members of the gangs revolted. An insurrection began in the month of September and political authorities of the town failed in their attempt to put it under control. At that time, the plot of Santo Domingo was put in execution. Former members of the disbanded army joined the group that enlarged substantially to attain the size of an invasion force. Armed with automatic rifles and moving with 4*4 vehicles under the command of Guy Philippe and Louis Jodel Chamblain, the rebels penetrated Haiti from the Dominican border. Aristide government was still popular and could maintain order. Cap Haitian, second town of the country fell under rebels hands and after they drove to merge with the rebels of Gonaives, the country was almost cut in two parts like it used to happen during the 19ᵗʰ century. The situation was like that when in the night of February 29, 2004; the world was informed that Aristide left the country. Two days later, he said the truth to the World: a commando embarked him in the middle of the night to exile in Africa.

The kidnapping: new tactical for the Haitian mob

Once again, Haiti has lost its national sovereignty. That time, we were under the control of a United Nation force. A new de facto government succeeded to Aristide. The president resided in the country and the prime minister was imported from the Diaspora. Before the newly installed government takes decision, a new trend appeared in Haiti: the kidnapping. During the two years of Latortue as prime minister, the phenomenon intensified. Thousands of qualified workers and executives fled the country and the economic situation degenerated. In order to solve the kidnapping and to calm down the social tensions, Haiti president maker, travelled to Marmelades to invite Rene Preval to succeed his mentor Aristide. The guess gave good result and Preval stabilized the country. We do not have the exact numbers of victims of the kidnapping, but we can state that phenomenon has now a profound impact in the social life of the country.

In this chapter, we have attempted a retrospective, which allowed us to learn the origin of some Haitian problems. This country will stay locked in political instability, unless the elites assume their responsibility. Our neighbors in the Caribbean enjoy relative peace allowing them to maximize their economic possibilities. Today, the social situation in Haiti is hopeless. The most important priority for our next generation of leaders will be to implement a favorable climate to a durable economic growth. We must include in the package a modernization of our judicial system and commercial while promoting free concurrence. Our ability to prove to investors that they can make profits In Haiti can revive the national production over the long term, which will lift thousands out of absolute poverty.

RENE PREVAL: THE MAN OF THE LAST DECADES.

In January 1991, the political world of Haiti received coolly the nomination by Aristide of Rene Preval as his prime minister. His landslide victory put him in excess of confidence, and Aristide decided to break early the ties with his associates of the National Front Of Convergence (FNCD). The first information that filtered on that unknown prime minister designated presented him as an underground militant of the democratic sector. He is from a family of the old aristocracy landowner of Marmelades, small town on the way to Cap Haitian. His father was a minister under the military regime of Paul Magloire in the 1950s. Under Francois Duvalier, he had to flee the country because of the repression-taking place at that time, especially for a son of a former Magloire minister. Everyone who collaborated with Paul Magloire became automatic enemy of Francois Duvalier. They said he went in Europe to Study agronomist at the University of Louvain, Belgium, but never graduated. Later, Aristide revealed that he picked Preval because of his political fidelity to him, he was a good follower.

During his recognition speech, he had not presented a clear political plan to solve the problems of the country. Many visible signs of tension could be seen inside the alliance who took the power and Preval did not show any management skills to solve the problems. He fired a large number of low-level public employees with no reason. The local of a union (CATH) was attacked and burned down in broad day light. Then it was the coup of September 30, 1991 and Preval went into exile in Washington with Aristide.

After the return of October 15, 1994, Rene Preval kept a low profile but remained very active among the base of Lavalas. In spite of all, he needed the benediction of Aristide to win the election of November 1995. We have to mention the low rate of voters in that election marked by the absence of any prominent figure of the opposition. Preval won easily the election but he never had a political base on his own. As a result, he never had a strong leadership over his own administration. Many observers of Haitian politics said at that time the true power of the country was in Tabarre. In addition, some people mention that for many nominations in the civil service, the last word had to come from Tabarre. Finally, Aristide made a spectacular move by creating a new party labeled "fami Lavalas". The division was consumed and the platform of Lavalas (OPL) had to choose a new name (organization of fighting people). Gerard Pierre Charles became the secretary General. They said Aristide is an autocrat who likes only to deal with subalterns. The separation affected the parliament and the public administration. Many organizations reputed close to Aristide kept organizing public manifestation against the economic reforms of the Preval Government. The Finance minister, Fred Joseph, had publicly claimed that he is a follower of the neoliberal policy. After the early resignation of Rony Smart, Preval governed the country by decree for a long time.

Finally, Jacques Edouard Alexis became prime minister and it was almost too late. The killing of the journalist Jean L Dominique, owner of a popular radio station during the fight against the duvalierist dictatorship was the sign that the Lavalas party was profoundly divided. He was a close adviser of Rene Preval and godfather of Aristide first child. A few months before his assassination, he denounced in an editorial broadcasted the senator Danny Toussaint who has sent people to manifest in front of radio Haiti Inter owned by Jean Dominique. It was not the first political killing during Preval tenure. Mireille Durocher Bertin, father Jean Pierre Louis, pastor Antoine Leroy, senator Guito, many high ranked officers of the disbanded army and many low-level persons renowned duvalierists were assassinated in what appeared as the acts of a serial killer.

In November 2000, election was held in spite of the boycott of the opposition and Aristide was elected easily President for the second time. Rene Preval stepped out in the silence of his native town of Marmelades until his resurrection in 2006. When the election was announced, nobody predicted the emergence of Rene Preval to the political power again. The opponents of the convergence who contributed to the fall of Aristide were getting ready to enjoy the dividends of their hard work. As always, some traditional political figures announced their candidacy: Marc Bazin, Hubert Deronceray, Lesly Manigat etc. In a surprising move, the candidacy of Rene Preval was announced under a party labeled "hope". It was a kind of platform grouping deceived Aristid supporter, some opportunistic and some beneficiaries of Preval first term. He will reveal later that some persons came to his hometown of Marmelades to praise to be their candidate in the new election. He is a character of division and a controversial political figure, Rene Preval is going to change prime minister twice, all of them close friends or long time ally. Each time, he finds a way to fire them. During his second term, corruption attained the level of indecency in the public administration. A number of natural disasters: successive hurricanes, landslides, and finally the January 12, 2010 earthquake, have turned Preval as the most unfortunate of all Haitian Presidents. At the inauguration of his presidency, he announced the withdrawal of the Minustah soldiers in Haiti, but before the end of his tenure, he became strong supporters of the occupation and patriots are being assassinated for demanding the end of the occupation. It is in such political conjuncture that Rene Preval wanted to name his successor. That time the magic has not worked for him and a novice to the Haitian political mess, a musical singer only famed for his dirty words and his dancing mannerism has been elected to the presidency.

I want to apologize to the readers for that long stay inside the political conflicts that marked Haitian politic since independence. I think it was important for the understanding of the problematic of the Haitian society. A country with two nations cannot survive. A country without responsible elites cannot progress. Some leaders whose patriotism must be questioned have marked the last decades. On May 14, 2011 when Rene Preval will pass the presidential banner to Michel Martelly, he will become the 56th president legally elected to lead the country. In 207 years of independence, we have known 78 governments of which 22 have occupied de facto the power representing an average of a government every 2 and half years. Among the legally elected Presidents, two were killed while in power and seven have terminated their mandate because the country was under military occupation. Seven of our presidents were dead while in power. Twenty-three went into exile after being overthrown from power. Only four Presidents could terminate their mandate and stay in the country without foreign occupation, that case is so rare that we judge necessary to mention their names: Nissage Saget, Tiresias Sam, Stenio Vincent and Rene Preval. We have had three American occupations (1915, 1994, and 2004) and before the proclamation of the result of the last election in April 2011, marines were already in the country under the pretext to help us for the hurricane season. The concept of national sovereignty does not exist anymore in Haiti. We would be lucky to be an American colony because colons and colonized finish by being linked over the long term. Like an American leader said it before the first occupation of 1915: "that nation of former slaves represent a public nuisance to our doors".

As of January 1, 1804

Products	Unite/ Millions	1989- 1990	1990- 1991	1991- 1992
Matches	Bout	35.093	21134	21.551
Beers	Bout	3958.8	4887	3281.2
Kola	Tones			
Sugar	Gallons	30.4		
Melissa	Tones	1.4		
Cement	Tones	265.3	211	106.4
Clinker	Tones	114.9	172.7	91.7
Cigarettes	Unites	963.5	1101.9	897.8
Tissue/cotton	Yards			
Tissue/Fiber	Yards			
OILs/ess	Kilos	190	112.1	111.8
OILs/com	Tones	80.8	105	95.3
Saindoux	Tones	7.4	10.6	6.6
Soap/lessive	Tonnes	43.9	49	34

Soap/toilette	Tonnes	0.6	1.9	0.6
Detergents	Kilos	1287.5	1214.6	912.7
Margarine	Kilos	2740.9	1546.8	1470.9
Electricity	Watts	535	491.2	347
Flour	Tonnes	106.2	62.2	11.6
		4992.3		

Source BRH-Direction des Etudes Economiques(October, 1993)

INDICE ANNUEL DE LA PRODUCTION INDUSTRIELLE
PAR BRANCHE D'ACTIVITES
1987-1988 A 1991-92

BRANCHES D'ACTIVITES	1987-88	1988-89	1989-90	1990-91	1991-92
	Column1	Column1	Column1	Column1	Column1
INDUSTRIES FOOD					
INDUSTRIES DU SUCRE	124.5	100.04	111.62	107.71	98.27
Beverages & Tobaco					
TEXTILE/Shoes	80.69	108.11	113.16	114.99	99.87
MINERAL/NON METALLIC					
INDUSTRY CHEMICAL	109.9	100.06	82.81	91.92	69.21
INDUSTRY DIVERSE					
TOTAL	102.45	106.12	104.14	99.11	88.12

SOURCE: BRH-DIRECTION DES ETUDES ECONOMIQUES-OCTOBRE 1993

EXPORTATIONS DES INDUSTRIES D'ASSEMBLAGE

EN MILLIERS DE DOLLARS

TYPE OF PRODUCTS	1987-88	1988-89	1989-90	1990-91	1991-92
TULLES	1845.6	1792	1856	2542.7	2027
EQUIPMENT	0	0	0	0	0
RADIO RECEIVER	73.072.6	59405	46093	40463	7679
MACHINE & ACCESSORIES	895	685.9	610.9	853.2	
ARTICLE OF TRAVEL	11364	9257.8	9642.6	12935	2396
CLOTHING	136.415	114.535	108.043	146.538	68.121
SOCKS	1.218.8	1500	1698.8	4298.7	1153
GAME/ SPORT ARTICLE	47700	38169	33771	26485	11445
PLASTICS ARTICLE	10422	7972	8023	5886	991
OPTICAL APPAREL	26071	21050	14868	9406	597
TOTAL	**98.434**	**139946.2**	**116671.3**	**103016.1**	**26356.12**

SOURCE: BRH-Economic Department-October 1993

The above tables show the bad outcomes of the three years Embargo on the Haitian economy.(1991-1994)

CHAPTER II

Restructuring our Education model

No country in the World can move on the road of progress without a well-educated population. In order to maximize the production function, a specific dosage of resources material, financial, and human must be mixed. A glimpse at the world economy confirms that education is at the start of economic progress. At each step of our evolution in the planet, the level of education pushes forward the system allowing scientific discoveries to change the status quo.

Disparities between classes

Since Haiti became a nation, a huge gap has always existed among the social classes interacting in the new society. In one side was the mulatto elite very well educated and on the other side the vast majority of uneducated Negroes, former slaves. The education level has served as a mean to move upward socially. In the 19th and 20th century, the education gap has widened because the wealthy parents, mulattoes in majority, sent their children in European Universities. Eventually, at their comeback, the public function belonged to them. A slogan of the liberal party required << the power to those who have the most ability >>, meaning the most educated. Born from white fathers and black mothers, the mulattoes benefited with a solid education.

The cast system installed by the colons put them in second place in the society as "Affranchis". As a result, the first executive of the Haitian administration were mulattoes. They had an advantage at the beginning on the other ethnic group. The grand mass of uneducated Negroes and formers slaves will constitute the class of peasants or the country outside. The recognition of Haiti independence by Paris in 1825 broke our international isolation. Nevertheless, the country had to wait until the agreement of 1860 signed with the Vatican to see Paris sent in the former colony a bunch of teachers. That period marked the presence of the Christian Brother for instruction (FIC) who have educated generation of Haitians including, students, teachers, professors, and universitarians. The number of catholic schools grew from two to fifty-two in 30 years. The only teachers were Brothers and Sisters from France who provided an education comparable to everywhere in the World. Next to the Catholic Church, the African Methodists, the Baptists, and the Episcopal opened their schools in Haiti. Enrollment in public and private schools peaked at 55.000 pupils about 15% of the school age population around 1910.

French Vs Creole

The school supervised by the missionaries assumed an education taught in French, the official language of Haiti. The class of "Affranchis "or now mulattoes spoke French as their primary language. Traditionally Haitians like to say that the French language is for the elite. In the other side, the mass of slaves, the poor of the new state used Creole as their official language. They became progressively a large mass of illiterates unable to communicate in the official language of their country transformed as a social barrier for them. Until now in Haiti, someone who has not ended the secondary cycle has less chance to succeed socially. Willing to put a distance between classes the government of Jean Pierre Boyer published a rural code in 1826. This act was at the base of the revolution of 1843 against Boyer.

Lack of funds to invest in Education

At the beginning, proponents of education constituted a natural broad-based group in the political class. The 150 million paid to France represented a burden so heavy for the young nation that education was competing with agriculture, public work, health and other national needs along the way, even though failing short on issues of quality raised by the factions. Haiti moved gradually from having no schools at independence time to one of the best schools system in the Caribbean. Haitian family accorded high importance to education, because of the opportunities for learning and upward socioeconomic mobility it provided their children, for most because of the social insurance and income that schooling contributed to their survival.

In the Northern department of the country, King Henry Christophe opened many primary and secondary schools between 1806 and 1816. Until recently, in the colleges of the Capital Port au Prince, students of northern origins tended to have better results than the other part of the country.

In the South Alexander Petion did almost the same. He opened many primary and secondary school, among them the High school bearing his name, which exists still today. The pressure exerted by Charles X who sent many warships in the Bay of Port au Prince had forced Boyer to accept the indemnity of 150 millions of Francs. That huge some will be paid back to colons that lost their assets during the war of independence. Since then, efforts made by his predecessors slowed down and schooling rate started declining in the country.

Education under the Occupation

During the first occupation of Haiti, the Americans have built many schools in Port au Prince and in the provinces. They created a lot trade and vocational schools where skills could be obtained without formal education. In addition, participants received a technical formation in agriculture. Enrollment in such program grew from 825 in 1924 to 11,400 in 1929. The occupants could not teach Haitians leader their role to educate the population. Since the constitution promulgated in 1805, all the following has always claimed education as a national priority. However, no government so far has assumed the follow up

Every year the Haitian educative system flows into the market thousands of bachelors ready for Universities. One time in Montreal, they were more Haitians doctors than in Haiti. In Mexico, many Haitians doctors work as practitioner. In Miami, New York, Boston, thousands of Haitians work professionally after leaving Haiti. Specially, in the field of Education Haitian has established a network inside the Board of Ed of New York. In the meantime, the rate of illiteracy has not decreased significantly in Haiti. Until now, in some remote rural areas, they do not have schools. The long distances to walk transform attending school as an exhausting exercise. Those who arrive to complete the cycle in such conditions must move out in another town to attend the secondary cycle. Moreover, the education system in Haiti is victim on the centralization administrative. Everything depends on the Education ministry in Port au prince, from a security guard to the departmental director.

Education and Demography

In the last decades, all Haitian government has recognized the right to educate the people. However, the big paradox is that the Haitian education system is private up to 90%. The state of poverty affects the level of education. In spite of some efforts during the last decades, the illiteracy rate stays above 50%. The lack of trained teachers is another crucial problem. The Haitian population speaks two languages: Creole and French. At the end of the secondary cycle, many schoolchildren and pupils do not speak French well. I agree with those who think that we should use Creole to teach French. In addition, I think that French must be seen as a mean of communication and not a scale to social promotion.

The demographic explosion of the last decades has carried also more problems for the education system. The migration from the provinces to the capital has lead to an increase in the demand of children ready to attend schools. As a result, a phenomenon called < school borlette > meaning overcrowded schools appears like a new problem to solve. The education ministry delivers license to teach too easily. The facts are clear. The education system is not preparing the way for an economic development. Do not forget that many researchers have proved that education and economic growth are positively related. A short visit in some schools of Port au prince can show the contradiction: some of them are fully computerized while in others the schoolboys and girls have not yet access to a computer. During the first American occupation of Haiti, the inequality to attend schools was reduced. When leaving the country, they were a new middle class with doctors, nurses, and technicians in other areas. I want to suggest to future Haitian leader to fix the education at the base first. They should begin by the primary cycle. The country needs new schools in the nine departments and the primary cycle must be free. At the secondary cycle, improvements can be provided. In this cycle, we have to adjust the system to be less theoretical. Why do we need to ask a student to be tested simultaneously in Haitian and in French literature at an official exam? We must introduce the system of electives classes in order to allow the student to have more choices.

At the primary cycle, in the public schools at least a meal should be distributed. At the secondary cycle, the school schedule should be standard. For example, some schools work twice a day while others work from 8am to 1pm. In addition, I would advise a zoning system, that is to say the public school will recruit in priority students residing in the area. For example, the chance to meet two students one from Carrefour and the other from Delmas in the same school has to be very low. That will permit partly to solve the transportation problem that I have seen in Port au Prince.

Today many Haitian professional reside and work in the Diaspora, a proof of the inability of Haiti to employ the Graduated. We have nothing against studying up to the University. However, the education reform has to start from bottom. The cost of higher education is increasing. It is very sad for a poor nation like Haiti to form students that will have to leave abroad. We must adjust our education system to the need of an underdeveloped economy. In the 1980s, many sub-contract factories had to move to Mexico, Panama because they could not find the qualified working-class in Haiti. At the same time, the University system in Haiti was flowing into the market, lawyers, managers, diplomats.

The private sector in Haiti must participate in the continuing education of his entry level employee. The modernization of the education system will be profitable to all sectors... In small country like Haiti, the private sector does not assume their responsibility. The government has to take charge for everything. The neoliberal's economic has proved that the private sector is more efficient than the public. The problem of clienteles in the public sector still affects the results. In the chapter about the necessity to reallocate the budget, I have mentioned the waste provoked by so-called center of formation. Why do we have to spend money for a school of financial management (ENAF)? The National institute of Haiti, the Economic Faculty and the businesses school of the private universities are able to provide young recruits for entry-level position in the Finance Ministry. I also remarked allocation for a school called National School for Hotelier. Is it the duty of the Haitian government to prepare employee for the hotel sector in the country? I think the Finance Ministry needs to take a close look and be realistic with the budget allocation.

When our government promises education for all, it implies that the State is prepared to assume all the cost. According to the last report by the Haitian Institute Of Statistics and Informatics (IHSI), the sector education in Haiti is under the control of private persons at 90%. In addition, 75% of that 90% of private schools are not under the control of the Haitian Education Ministry. Now, the big question is how the Haitian government will provide free primary education for all children before 2015. The demographic explosion favors the construction of new schools in the cities. While driving on the road of Carrefour, south of Port au Prince, one can see a school every two blocs. There is no space for the students because the rooms are too small for the number of admitted. They are at least 15.000 young Haitians studying in the Dominican Republic. Because of that, Leonel Fernandez, Dominican president has given a University Campus to Haiti.

To conclude, I think that the education problem in Haiti must be tackle in the context of our poverty. We are agreeing to place Education among the high priorities of the country, however, others problems such as the demographic explosion, our incapacity to nourish the population, the economic stagnation, and the eternal political conflicts must also be taken seriously. The reform of education in Haiti goes further, we must think about a new social contract. The improvement of the justice system, the deforestation, the undesired pregnancies can benefit from a population more educated.

CHAPTER III

An agriculture of poverty.

The history of the world is also the one of agriculture. The cavern men suffered of malnutrition because at that time technology was not yet under control. . The need of food pushed the first inhabitants of the planet to adopt a sedentary way of life. Then, little by little, men started to dominate the nature and lived from hunting and fishing. Before the industrial revolution took place in England, the entire world lived from farm products. Today, agriculture still represents an important economic sector in most underdeveloped countries.

On December 6, 1492 when Columbus conquered that island inhabited by Karibe Indians, he decided to name it, Hispaniola. The genial navigator was stone by the similarity of the Island with Spain. They said he liked the green climate of the new conquest. However, the exploitation of golden mines was the first target of the Conquerors. Columbus and his men imposed an infernal rhythm of work to the native and only a few of them will survive. From 1503, the Spaniards went on the coastal of West Africa to buy prisoners of wars from fighting African tribes. For alcoholic beverages such as rum and liquors, they bought slaves to be transported to the Americas and the Caribbean. Like animals, these human beings were travelled nude by boat. That was the beginning of a commerce, which will last at least five centuries. Historians report that the majority of slaves sold in Haiti came from Benin, Guinea, and from the Goree island of Senegal. Because of the rivalry opposing the super power of that moment, Haiti alternately became possession of Spain, British and French.

Finally, in 1697, with the Ryswick treaty the island was split in two: the East to the Spanish, the West to the French. The metropolis sent from Paris the best engineers to develop the agriculture of the island. Around 1742, the sugar production of Saint Domingue was higher than all the British colonies reunited. By 1789, the commerce between French and Saint Domingue doubled in dollars value the exchange between England and its thirteen colonies in America. The French built a modern irrigation system. The principal products exported to Paris were sugar, coffee, cotton and woods. The political events of the metropolis echoed in the colony. With the ceremony of "bois caiman "in August 1791, a slave uprising against the system will finish until the colony declared its freedom from French.

During the war of independence, the infrastructure put in place by the French was destroyed and the prosperity of Saint Domingue declined. Once the colons left, the rest of the plantation was transformed in ruins. The system of large property was going to be transformed because of the large distribution of land organized by the government who took power after the Killing of Jean Jacques Dessalines. Everyone wanted to have its small part of the land. Since that time agriculture in Haiti was done for survival. The peasants work to satisfy their family needs, and the surplus is sold to the market. The former slaves were not interested to work even for money in the large properties. In their small properties, the peasants try to cultivate everything. All year long, the family needs will be satisfied. What is left is transported to the market.

The agrarian question was the first cause of conflicts in the newly independent State.

The murder of Dessalines on October 17, 1806 was the outcome of a conflict opposing the olds General winner of the independence war and the mass of old slaves now free men. The cast system in the colony of Saint Domingue divided the population in three groups: White, Affranchis (mulattoes and free blacks), slaves (blacks only). In the absence of the white, the army General mostly mulattoes monopolized the goods left by the former colons. The Emperor who decided to find a solution to the complaints of mass newly freed from slavery. He attempted to use the big stick and the result was his killing. This crime had not resolved the land conflict in Haiti. The trend of dividing the large property in small lands became a mean used by Presidents to satisfy their clienteles. A new President has to make distribution of lands to attire new followers for the support of the regime. Alexandre Petion was called << father with a Great Heart >> because his laissez faire attitude in the distribution of land. In spite of all, this method of distribution could not satisfy everybody. In 1843, Jean Jacques Acau took the leadership of peasants without lands and claimed a redistribution of the ones owed by the State. In the North, the monarchy of Christophe kept the system of large properties. Many skirmishes opposed the Army of the King with the peasants who refused to work in the large properties. One of our famous independence warriors, Francois Capois called "Capois la mort "was killed by Christophe because he rebelled against his policy. When the King was dead, Jean Pierre Boyer became a President for the entire island and keeps doing the distribution of land to his partisans.

The American occupation (1915-1934)

Before the American occupation of Haiti in 1915, the peasants abandoned by the power of Port au Prince started living Haiti toward other countries principally Cuba and the Dominican Republic. While the political leaders (black and mulatto) were fighting for the power in Port au Prince, the agricultural productivity of Haiti declined. The erosion in the mountains reduces the land productivity and the peasants without lands escaped to the neighborhood countries. The presence of the occupants will not improve the situation for the peasants. The lack of funds for the rebuilding of roads and bridges pushed the marines to apply an old practice dated during the colonial era. In that system named <<corvee>>, the peasants had to work in roads construction to avoid paying taxes. Thanks to the "corvee", the Americans forced the peasants to construct a road of 170 miles connecting Port au Prince to Cap Haitian. . Rapidly, the complaints of peasants could be heard. The "corvee" appeared offensive to the peasants because it reminded them of the old slavery method. They were many massacres. A great number of peasants went into hiding in the mountains, many of them to rejoin the guerillas Cacos under Charlemagne Peralte leadership. In spite of the interdiction of the "corvee" by the marines commanders, in the North of the country the practice was maintained. The result of the 19 years of American occupation raised many controversies. In spite of the American advance in agriculture, Haiti did not benefit of technological transfer. In certain parts of the country, peasants categorically denied the assistance because of the racist attitude of the occupants.

THE JAMES P MC DONALD COUP.

Saint Domingue was made famous by its agricultural productivity. The decision by a consortium of American investors to build a network of rail way linking different parts of the country was at that epoch the right move for Haiti' s economic takeoff. According to the contract, the firm will build a road of 40 miles through the plaine du cul de sac by 1904. A Germanic firm took control of the first contract. The Haitian government gave a second concession, this time an American investor, James McDonald signed the deal. Unfortunately, the contract of Mc Donald will cost the Haitian nation a lot of money, which could have been used in the payoff of the debt to French.

The official date of the concession was April 1910, and the Haitian State had to guaranteed bonds issued at $ 33.000 for each mile built in the rail way. In addition, the contract gave to

McDonald 19 kilometers of land on both sides of the railway to cultivate bananas for which he received a monopoly to export. The rail way should link Port au Prince to Cap Haitian passing through Saint Marc, Gonaives and Ennery. The American executive will default the contract. On purpose, he transferred his rights of concession to the First National City Bank. In 1914, The American claimed they have finished the job. Less than half of the work was done and City Bank maintained his claims on the Haitian government. That is why Roger Fahrnam, PDG of City Bank will take part in the decision of the State Department to intervene in Haiti. Eventually, the 90 miles unfinished of the network will be reimbursed to the City Bank at $33.000 per miles. The payment of that swindle will extend to the Government of Elie Lescot. The Coup of McDonald must be inserted among the abuses perpetrated against the poor Haitian nation. Beside of our perpetual conflicts for land distribution, cases of fraud like that have prevented the Haitian nation to progress. We had a fantastic debt to repay and our agriculture had a surplus to be exported. The building of that rail way could have provoked an economic boom in the North of the Island. An increase of our exports at that time would have had a multiplier effect on the Haitian economy overall. Instead of that, we had to pay money for an unfinished job.

We have already completed a decade in the 21st Century. Instead of improving, the Haitian poverty has become worst. In April 2008, riots took place in Port au Prince because of hunger. The increase in price of almost all the base products of consumption has forced many poor to invade the streets. They were casualties and lost in human life and the damaged were very important. In spite of that, we do not have the impression that our leaders have understood the true cause of that event: the continuing fall of agricultural productivity in Haiti. To make it easier for our readers, we are going to investigate inside the different factors preventing an increase of agricultural output.

A) The reduction in the agricultural space.

Haiti is a small country of 27.750 square kilometers. Published data in CIA fact book in 2003 stated that Haiti should count 438.000 squares of cultivable lands. More than half of that area is constituted with arid slopes called "morns ". The irregular cut of trees in the mountains has lead to a progressive erosion of those lands. Today only 2% of Haiti total superficies have trees and forests. In the lowland, the demographic explosion and the need to build new houses reduce the farmers 'area to plant. The newly build constructions in the "Plaine du cul de sac "food basket of Port au Prince are the perfect sample of that space reduction. Driving though the country allows the observers to notice the same phenomenon in many cities. Some large spaces of agricultural lands are being sacrificed to house construction. In other words, the urbanization of our cities is becoming a long-term threat to our agriculture. I think that the mayors of the cities have to address that concern.

A) **Non-existing Property title**.

Since the killing of Dessalines because of the verification of property titles he tried to do, no Haitian government has resolved the problem. The lands are transferred by heritage without title. That state of anarchy has existed for more than 200 years. The former president Jean Bertrand Aristide created the national institute for agrarian reform (INARA) with mission to solve the problem of property titles in Haiti. By the way, Aristide could not have resolved anything because he never had a chance to lead the country.

B) **Location of Lands and sharecropping**

In Haiti, each government brings his newly rich people. Depending on his contact inside the new government, a peasant can rent a land from the state and put some other peasants to plant the land. The sharecropper or two halves is another form of exploitation use in

Haiti. In this case, the renter of the land is absent and comes back only to harvest half of the total production. According to an estimate, 90% of all agricultural plantations in Haiti are less than 3 hectares. The large property has always been in the subconscious of Haitian farmers a slave thing.

C) **Technical backwardness**

More than 4 centuries after the industrial revolution, it is unacceptable that the Haitian peasants are still using machetes and hoes to prepare lands. Those outdated methods reduce productivity and destroy the soil. The watering of farm is so expensive that only a few peasants can afford it. The poor peasant has to rely on the rainy season. The modernization of the Haitian Agriculture constitutes a big challenge for our next leaders. According to Andre Gunderfrank, agriculture represents the only exit for the poorest countries.

D) **Inexistence of a clear agricultural policy.**

I researched deeply in the kind of agricultural policy conducted by our leaders for the last 50 years; I have realized that none of them had really given a priority to it. The regime of Jean Claude Duvalier adopted three five-year plans for agriculture from 1971 to 1986. , but they did not obtain the results. From the last American intervention in Haiti reinstating Aristide to power until now, our agriculture underwent a disaster.

THREE SUCCESSIVE PLANS.

The Electric power plant of Peligre newly built allowed an increase in the energy capacity of the country. The irrigation of lowlands under control of the Organization of Development of the Artibonite valley (ODVA) and the rice plantations of low Artibonite had been solved. The plan designer thought finding the miracle solution to increase the agricultural output. They wished to increase the output of some based products, but they fell short of the expected growth. An average of 2 % increase in the productivity resulted in five years.

1976-1981

The new plan was created on the path of the old. That time the technician could observe the reason of their failure and brought the corrections. In their new approach, they wanted to go further in the rural section. Some projects like the Development Regional Integrated of Petit Goave and Petit Trou (DRIPP) was created. They envisaged the creation of a growth pole, which through the multiplier effect could generate a durable increase in the agricultural productivity. They expected a yearly rate of 5%. However, to the end of the fifth year, a new failure was registered. The average increase never crossed 2.5%.

1981-1986

During our history, no government has ever received international support than the one of Jean Claude Duvalier. In spite of the failure of the first two plans, the international community advised the technicians of the National Council of Development (CONADEP) and a third plan was brought on. The Canadian government who was financing the DRIPP project stopped giving their money. Uprisings in Raboteau in 1984 warned of the failure of Agriculture in the country.

What is the explanation for the successive failure of three plans? The international experts advising the Haitians have rebuked the lack of enthusiasm of the government to finance their compensation. The problems of the land system in Haiti constituted another reason of the failure. Most of Haitian large properties do not have legal papers and still no new land plan for the country. The systematic uses of corruption and favoritism played an important role in the failure. The big fellow of the Duvalier regime took loans at the BNDAI, they never repaid

them, and the bankers had no way to collect the bad debts from
macoutes. In spite of all, based on numbers, our researches allow
to conclude that was the best moments of Haiti's economy.

In an article of the daily news paper < Le nouvelliste > dated
July 2009, one can read the World Bank has approved a donation
of $5 millions to Haiti to reinforce the management of agricul-
ture in the country for a durable development. The donation is
inscribed in the framework of program to intervene as a way to
respond to the food crisis worldwide, (GFRP), worked out by the
World Bank last year, according to a note of the Bank website.

That project wants to sustain the reform of the public sector
in Haiti, declared Yvonne Tsikata, World Bank director for the
Caribbean. It is the first step in the resumption of operations
with Haiti in this domain, for agriculture is the key sector in the
rural economy and a source of growth for the poor.

Agriculture still plays a role important in the Haitian economy. That sector carries 25% of the national GDP and about 50%
of jobs in rural area, thus maintaining 75% of poor. During last
year, hurricanes and fluctuation of prices of based products have
weakened the agricultural sector and his political institutions.
The new project of the World Bank aims to help the agriculture
ministry to put in hierarchy and target the investments function
of the agriculture policy, and to improve the local services of
assistance to the agricultural sector.

The total amount of donations given by the World Bank to
Haiti since January 2005 is about 273 millions of dollars. The
Bank has approved on June 3, a total amount of 121 million of
dollars for its new aid assistance strategy (2009-2012). Some 29
millions of Dollars were given as fiduciary resources.

What are doing the staff of Damiens and the planning ministry? They should apply the article 248 of the 1987 constitution
creating the INARAH. Without deep changes in our agrarian
structure, the increase in output will not be possible. China and
India are the two examples of countries taking off after agricultural reform.

CASE FOR INCREASING CREDIT TO THE AGRICULTURE

On the World Bank advices, the former Finance ministry of the National council of government, Leslie Delatour, adopted a package to encourage economic growth. He decided to close down the BNDAI, the lowering of customs tariff for many products and the lifting of import ban on others. The obtaining of credit is not easy in Haiti. For a peasant, obtaining a loan in a private Bank is a fiction. The BNDAI has represented the only way for a peasant needed cash to buy seeds. Otherwise, a private lender will give loans at very high interest rate. Why did that minister cut the main source of credit for peasants? I assisted at a debate in the Science faculty between that ministry and the agronomist Jean Jacques Honorat. The latter wanted to mention the damages he was doing to the Haitian agriculture. As I can remember, his responses were not clear. As a ministry, he could not give any rationale to sustain his decision. In front of the protest of the young participants, he closed the debate because he said he was in a hurry. The curtain went down in the room and on the poor peasants of the valley and mountains of the singular Republic. We have made that reminder because we believe in the microcredit to help Haitian agriculture. The success of Mohamed Yunus with Gramen bank in Bangladesh proves that microcredit can work. Indeed, in Haiti analphabetism is still a handicap for the peasant to get a credit index, for they are not able to fill in the paper work.

NECESSITY FOR AN AGRICULTURAL PLAN.

We have to go back from 1980 to 1986 to clean the disorder of bad policies in the calamities that destroyed all the Haitian pigs and promoted export crops instead of agricultural food. During the last years, the rules dictated by the World Bank, IMF and USAID have advised some strategy based on exportations of products that are responsible for our actual problems. To find money for their own, the macoutes of Duvalier had overtaxed the exports of agricultural products from 1957 to 1984. The fiscal policy of Duvalier included the taxes on foods being exported, the excise taxes and the non-fiscal accounts of the Regie du Tabac et des Allumettes representing from 1968 to 1973 an annual average of 24% of State revenue from Agriculture while the government was spending only 7.5% in the agricultural sector for the same period. This trend had increased because in 1984, rural Haiti furnished 55% of public revenue but received only 13% of public spending. That taxation policy reduced the peasants to poverty. To avoid the taxes the peasants used what some Haitians scholars called " economic marronage " which consisted in farming only the less taxable crops. After the elimination of the market tax on September 11, 1974, the peasants became interested only on the products they could sell in the local market.

The Haitian calamities had increased seriously by what some activists called "the American plan for Haiti "consisting in the reduction of investment in Agriculture. The Haitian economy that was based on the production of food crops will be reoriented toward some other products and the assembling industry. Coffee, which represented 35% of exports in 1968, dropped to 19% in 1984 while the assembling products climbed from 6.4% in 1970 to 35% in 1984. We are still paying the price of that transformation today. In addition, the food aid of PL-480 has consolidated that transformation definitely, in spite of the warning expressed by David Kinley in April 1986. The "American Plan resulted in a huge migration of persons from the provinces to Port au prince which population of 507.000 residents in 1971 augmented to 2 millions in 1990..

After the uprisings of April 2008, we heard that the Preval government was about to reopen the BNDAI. I had hope that we will start talking about increase in the agricultural productivity. More rejoicing was the news that the agricultural minister Jonas Gue was about to launch again the agricultural farms in the South. I think that this trend must stay even after the exits of Minister Jonas Gue. To support the small farms, I would recommend the production of food crops, fruits and livestock. The government should use its own land to increase the size of farm that can lead to an augmentation of output. In order to rationalize the agricultural space, the mountains would not be used for products that need to be weeded, but for fruits and pasture. In the valley, agriculture could have a food function and will be produced only food crops targeting only the local market. In addition, I think that the minimum wage should be applied for the agricultural workers.

In 2009, the US ambassador in Haiti, Ms Janet Sanderson officially launched a new project called "Marche". Targeting the domains where the Haitian population excels such as agriculture, art craft and tourism, "Marche "will invest an amount of 15 millions of dollars during the next 3 years. Through programs of formation, this new program of USAID wants to reinforce the abilities of association of planters, artisan, small farmers and merchants. The USAID will encourage the small and middle producers to improve their products in quality and quantity and will make easier the sale on the foreign and Haitian market. In his speech, Ambassador Janet Sanderson declared that through accompaniment process, agents of "Marche "will work with farmers association to help them to increase their production of rice, sweet potatoes, plantain, cacao and coffee. The agents of "Marche "will teach the mango producers how to improve the quality and quantity of their products. This project will aid farmers not only to increase their production, but also to sell them at reasonable price. Ambassador Sanderson put emphasized on the importance of alliances between the private and public sector in the reinforcement of micros, small, and middle firms, which will contribute to promote economic growth.

I also read in the Novelist that a former agricultural ministry was decorated for what he has done for the Haitian agriculture. Unfortunately, I have not had the chance to read or listen a listing of the achievement of that ministry. The hunger riots of April 2008 gave the proof of the failure of the agricultural policy in the country. I had also the chance to read two documents published by the planning ministry and external cooperation. These documents are very well done. With data from the nine department of the country, these documents should help the drawing up of a good economic policy for Haiti. Instead, I read that the planning ministry was going to adopt the "plan Collier ", a British economic teacher.

WHAT WILL BE THE EFFECTS OF THE EARTHQUAKE ON HAITI AGRICULTURE?

According to estimates after the earthquake, ½ million of persons left Port au prince to settle in rural Haiti. Let us remind that 29% of the 27.750 square mile of the country is arable land. The productive soils of Haiti are described by the small size of the plot of land. Approximately, 80% have a size between 1 & 1.8 ha. It is very probable that the pressure on the agricultural lands will increase with the migration from cities to the provinces. About 60% of the Haitian populations are living in rural area and 21% were residing in Port au Prince. Although the civil code mentions that land transactions must be signed and respected. In most cases, it does not happen. Almost 35% of rural lands in Haiti are not registered and 9% have only the receipt of the acquisition as proof. About 70% of land contract follow the rule. Then, the complexity of heritage rule regarding land possession is the cause of many conflicts among families. Haitian peasants generally acquire their land through heritage or by buying it. The rules of succession make it more difficult and aggravate the cases of breaking up. The National Institute of Agrarian Reform (INARA) is an institution creates to solve land problems in the country. However, that agency has not been able until now to fulfill his goal concerning the title and the needs of the country for the access to land because of the lack of coordination among governmental agencies, technical difficulties to adjust the land plan and the deficiency in human and financial resources.

The goal regarding the security of land has two objectives: one is to secure the land ownership in the rural area with an equitable process, transparent and legal, and somewhere else, to favor the access to land by agreements culturally acceptable, which can stimulate agricultural growth and investments for the well being of rural communities.

PROGRESSIVE EROSION AND EXCESSIVE BREAKING UP OF LAND.

To vanquish the obstacle of land ownership in rural Haiti, there is actually a mean to consider a global approach responding to the short and long-term goal of agricultural development for the period 2010-2015.That new approach of land ownership can help the area with plenty of arable lands, such as irrigated valley, slopes and muggy lands. It is equally necessary that, in the midterm, the suggested approach solve the principal difficulties of land ownership encountered by the country nationally. That is why the approach has two phases: a short-term strategy to answer the insecurity of land possession and inherent problems linked to the small size of parcels in the irrigated zones and in the ones receiving the benefits of investments. After that, a midterm strategy consisting of a reform of rural ownership, integrating a policy of land possession, the revision of the legal context, a systematically land plan and registration of titles. In general, the institutional context, politic, and social of the country is not ready for structural intervention and deep in the land problem. However, giving security to those who owned the land is crucial to the productivity of the land. It is a sure way to conserve resources and to encourage investments in that sector.

Next to the Finance ministry, the direction of land conservation (ONACA), the national institutes of land reform (INARA) are agencies responsible of land ownership in the country. However, the difficulties of coordination in the country of all the agencies supervising the land questions, problems related to land have not been fixed. I suggest that our next leaders allow INARA to fulfill its role. That agency can help solve the old injustice problems of sharecropping and absenteeism of landowners. Moreover, the updating of legal means to fix the duration of rented land to avoid illegal and abusive increase in the price of sharecropping. The traditional agricultural way will not survive because of soil erosion, and the demographic explosion. A green revolution should be put in place besides of the technical help to the peasants. The use of burned woods as a source of energy should stop because it causes a permanent destruction of our forests. Let us remind that only 2% of Haiti territory now has forests. Without a modernization of our agricultural method of production and the forestation, Haiti agriculture will die slowly but surely. To conclude our analysis of the agricultural problems of Haiti, I want to mention that 60% of jobs in the country belong to that sector.

CHAPTER IV

Corruption and poverty in Haiti.

Corruption is a universal phenomenon to all nations. Before the birth of the Nation State, all form of authority needed to collect money to survive. In the time where the big cities dominated the world, taxes permitted to the Kings to live lavishly. Saint Thomas of Aquino has been canonized in spite of being a tax collector. By the way, that old saying was attributed to him :<< virtue necessitates a minimum of well being >>. The need to become rich pushed the Kings to finance the conquest of new land. French, England, Spain, and Portugal were fighting to take control of the wealth of the new continent of America, Africa, and Asia. Once landed the new masters imposed to the indigenous population hashed condition of work. That is why everywhere they went, it was genocide. In America after the decimating of the Indians race, European masters decided to replace them by imported Negroes from Africa. French and Spanish were the first to begin the importation after they realize the blacks adjust easily to the hard farm jobs. That form of exploitation leading to easy fortune of state at the expense of another. The two world wars in 1914 and 1945 have reduced that trend. Nevertheless, at the society level, exploitation and corruption still represent the oil for the engine of the capitalist system.

In what is our concern, in Haiti, corruption and exploitation of poor seem to be the reason of that State. After the premature birth of that nation, the founders could not make it work, Economic embargo and diplomatic isolation have jammed Haiti for two decades. The mulattoes, one of the two ethnic groups, which created the State, had the lion share in the economic plate. When Jean Jacques Dessalines wanted to put more equality in the system, he was murdered. The country was divided in two. The first decision of Alexander Petion was to impose new taxes. Customs became the cashier official of the Republic and the General Bonnet was the instigator of the fiscal package. At the difference of Dessalines, the new government increased more taxes on coffee than sugar. After the damages of the sugar plantations during the war of liberation, peasants planted coffee more than sugar. The army Generals took possession of most sugar plantation and the tax authority put a rate lower on sugar than coffee.

That type of corruption concerns mostly a predatory State, which reinforce the social inequality. The other aspect of corruption is the stealing of money by the head of State and his collaborators. We had the case of President Michel Domingue and his bogeyman Septimus Rameau who went to exile with suitcases full of cash money. Before that, Faustin Soulouque had used all the asset reserves of the country to be crowned Emperor. Tiresias Simon Sam fled the country in broad day light with suitcases full of money. President Cincinnatus Leconte disappeared in the fire provoked by the explosion of the Palace. Former president Trancrede Auguste who blamed Cincinatus for the process of consolidation planned the plot. Ulcerated by the embezzlement occurred during the work of asphalt of Port au Prince, after taking power Cincinnatus put on trial all the responsible of the project and many of them were condemned. We do not have many samples of such judgment in Haiti. During the first occupation of Haiti, corruption went down. The governments of Vincent, Lescot, and Estime were not marked by big cases of corruption. The lost of the contract with the Standard Fruit to exploit bananas in Haiti can be attributed to corruption of some Haitian legislators. They forced the administration of Estime to break the monopoly of the American Giant Firm specialized in Agriculture. However, the lack of expertise will lead to the extinction of the banana industry in Haiti. During the reign of Paul Magloire, the public claimed that his brother Arsene had plundered the Haitian treasury. They said that he put in his pocket a vast quantity of money from the project of installing private phone in Port au Prince and the construction of the hydroelectric barrage of Peligre. Francois Duvalier famous for his brutality succeeded in reducing fraud during his tenure. The suspension of the American aid to Papa doc put his regime in a bad financial situation. After Jean Claude Duvalier departure, many foreign Medias reported that he fled the country with 900 million dollars. Jean Bertrand Aristide was denounced by the American Media as an associate of the drugs cartels. However, up to now, no proof was advanced against the two former presidents. After Aristide departure, many persons in his entourage were indicted by the DEA (American Drug Enforcement). Under the second tenure of Rene Preval, the media denounced many cases of corruptions. An executive of the government, Marcelo was kidnapped because he refused to share deals in the management of market bid. The $197 million of Petro Caribe authorized to use by Venezuelan President Hugo Chavez after the four hurricanes of 2008 have disappeared. In the following conflict between Preval and Michele Pierre Louis, the Senate dismissed the latter.

Another aspect of the corruption I want to tackle is the public offices in Haiti. During my trips to Haiti, I inquired inside the administration and I found that corruption is still defying the administration. Facilitated by the weaknesses in the justice and security sector, this phenomenon represents an important obstacle in the improvement of governance, and economic growth. The Haitian public sector had some good results regarding transparency of the Budget entranceway of corruption. However, people I spoke with think that the payment of bribes for public transactions symbolized the corruption. It is an important source of corruption taking place in motor vehicle department and in the Customs administration. For some persons, the low salary of the agents and an inadequate system to denounce corruption count among the cause of embezzlements. Moreover, the use of political influence affecting justice decisions, the personal and the Budget is a continuing challenge to solve.

I made some research that confirmed that the persistence of bad governance is the reason of loss of money for the private firms and discourage some person in utilizing public services. That evil also harms the functioning of public institutions and ONG sector, and put a burden partially heavy on the poor and fragile Haitian society. In addition, the referral for quality services and the trust in the public sector are very low for many public agencies considered as dishonest or offering bad services.

A significant number of persons I have talked to mentioned that corruption is a very bad problem and indicated the problem became worst during the last years. If those revelations constitute a challenge, our inquiry gave us some detailed on how to reform the governance. Singularly, the civil society presents some champions of good governance: the Medias, and the religious institutions, which count among the most efficient contributors in the fight against corruption. The unit to fight corruption (ULCC), a State institution, plays an important role. The misfortune to signal corrupt activities have been equally studied. Families give as reason principal not to report cases of corruption the fact that nothing will happen after that, and they scared of retaliations. The agents are very dissuasive and the difficulties of knowing where to complaint see the fears of vengeances. These data advise specific areas where the government could increase surveillance to catch corruption.

The effect of recent political and economical difficulties of Haiti is reflected in the point of view of any person met in the streets. The vast majority think that their life quality is very bad. After the earthquake, they noted a worsening in the conditions of life in many domains such as health, education, and justice. That deterioration affects many sectors of the Haitian society but mostly the poor depending on public services. Nevertheless, the most ready to say that the quality of life has worsened are the people under the tents. The youths consider that unemployment, the cost of services and the lack of foods among their first preoccupation. Corruption in the public sector is qualified as a serious problem by a large number of agents. The numerous forms of corruption and the lack of efficiency are mentioned among the reason why the general situation has deteriorated. In the private sector, the lack of security is the main obstacle of growth followed by the kidnapping, crime, and inflation. Almost any executive will tell you that corruption is very bad in both sectors. The confidence level in the ability of the government to solve those problems is very low. Persons from all social classes think that the government is going in the bad direction and does not take care of the population need.

TYPE OF CORRUPTION.

The bribes are paid en general 10% of the transaction cost. The phenomenon of corruption in Haiti appears on different forms. Families, firm executives, and civil service employee confirm all that bribes to obtain good services influence judicial decision. They do not make bids to receive public contracts and even public jobs remain a permanent problem. Agents of the public sector declared that some of them knew about bribes. In addition, some cases involving local or international enterprises were the act of civil service agents. That type of corruption inside the government can constitute an obstacle to economic growth because it tends to discourage investors. Many firm executives explain that bribes to agents are necessary to obtain a public contract. However, a majority of public agent denies the existence of corruption to obtain contract. For that majority of agents only a small quantity of contracts was provided after bribes, and theses payments constituted a very low percentage of the contact costs. Some persons have confirmed giving bribes to receive basic services. They pointed the fingers at the motor vehicle and the customs office, while the frequency of bribes was a little significant in the justice ministry. The payment of bribes is evident in the decision of public agents involving in the Budget. The results indicate that employees of the justice ministry, customs office and TELECO demand the big bribes for a promotion. Corruption represents generally a material cost for the whole government because bribes are used to avoid paying taxes. Mostly the users of public services feel the financial cost of corruption. Many families and businesses tell they are ready to do a big effort to eliminate the practice of corruption.

SOUNDNESS OF HAITIAN INSTITUTIONS.

The private sector and the ONGS are agreed that the custom and the tax office are the most corrupt public offices in Haiti. The judicial system including the justice ministry and public security, the judges and tribunals, is seen as lacking integrity. That absence of integrity in the judicial system has been attributed to corruption inside the National Police. We have to underline that based on the trend of the answers; crime and violence are solid obstacles to the improvement of life quality in Haiti. The parliament and the political parties do not escape the phenomenon of corruption. The worst public services regarding integrity are TELECO, CAMEP, SNAP and EDH. In addition, many persons contacted gave bad notes to many others public services. The banking sector enjoys a high level of integrity and they are reputed for their good services. As a result, those examples of honesty should serve as model to influence another sector.

CORRUPTION AND PROMOTION IN THE HAITIAN CIVIL SERVICE.

The shortcomings in the public sector make it easy for corruption and constitute a key factor in the lack of integrity of public agents. Information collected show some serious problems of governance, our contacts have indicated that the public agencies still maintain some good procedures. Data show favorable boars for the recruitment of personal. The majority of agents confirmed they were hired on open tests or by internal promotion. Many agents think that the rules regarding management in their unit are very well applied. They admit that the recruitments are based on meritocracy and only a few talked about political pressure. Employee from commerce ministry and the tax office consider that competency pays in their institution.

Nevertheless, an important number of civil service employee pretend that recommendations of a friend or another insider played a role in their hiring process and some confirm they have been subjugated to the three months trial. Information on employment in the civil service depends on personal relationship. Almost all civil service employees in Haiti will tell you they heard about their job by notification of a friend. A very tiny minority of them will have listen to that by the media. For other agents, decisions regarding the staff were rarely transparent.

Certain public employees mentioned the condition of their recruitment associated to the bad moral of agents. A majority of agents would prefer to work in the private sector. Notwithstanding, agents of the public sector resign rarely to go to work in the private, the reverse is also infrequent. Generally, agents see the merit and seniority as determining factors of hiring in the public sector. However, speaking of other factors used for recruiting, most interlocutors talk about bribes. Some of them have mentioned family relation and political pressure.

THE JUSTICE SYSTEM FACES UP CORRUPTION.

Justice is a key element for good governance, but in Haiti, the beliefs are spread that the system is unfair and subject to the manipulation of powerful interests. That point of view illustrates a limited access to the justice system. Only a minority of citizens have indicated to appeal to tribunals during the last three years. Those who have been in court qualify unfavorably that experience. Data suggest that citizen have a limited access to the justice system. Almost all the persons who went to justice described the system as unfair. By the way, the vast majority of the population considers that the tribunals are discriminatory against the poor. According to an important average of managers, the government and powerful economic group manipulate the tribunal. In addition, NGO affirm that the judges are vulnerable to the threats when pronouncing judgments against powerful group. They have denounced many problems preventing the appeal to the justice system. For example, in many cases the decisions of the tribunals are not respected. The lateness of procedures and the lack of clarity of the law appear among the principals' deterrent factors mentioned by half of persons. These obstacles prevent or discourage people who really need the justice system. A large quantity of citizen has declared to avoid any appeal to the justice system even when they need to go to court to solve their problems. In many cases, people preferred to ask help from friends or a family member. Sometimes, they also addressed a religious chief or community.

CORRUPTION AND INSECURITY.

The entire group consulted says that the lack of security is the principal obstacle in the improvement of quality of life in Haiti. The NGO have defined the insufficiency of security as the second defy most important to access services and the executives have identified that situation as a serious obstacle to the growth of their activities. Many activists confirmed that the level of violence and crime has increased in the years following Aristide departure. Almost everyone I had the chance to talk during my visits in the country affirm to have at least one of their sibling's victims of violence. Our information shows us that corruption of the security forces and their efficiency to fight the insecurity are factors that emphasize the problem and source of bad governance inside the State. The respondents of all categories have mentioned that poverty as the principal causes of insecurity, however an average adds that the inefficiency of the National Police is one of the reasons of the persistency of the problem. Moreover, this lack of confidence in the Police force represents an obstacle to the access of services for many victims of violence. In reality, many victims of violence looked for help somewhere else. For many Haitians, citizens of Port au prince, the police are not able to improve security and others hope a comeback of the former Haitian Armed Forces. Good governance requires a systemic approach to improve the functioning of public institution. Although our researches have put in evidence the weak points inside the structure of the State, we have to note the way to improve performance; reforms are necessary at the level of users and performers of services. In Haiti, some people classify themselves and the State as the two agents contributing to corruption. We have to remark that customs agents and the police are classified as the worst among all the other agents. For many specialists, religious institutions, Medias, and NGO are efficient in the fight against corruption. NGO generally recognize the positive role of Medias and give them the first place in that domain. The unity fighting against corruption (ULCC) is more efficient than the government. Many friends told me that they do not believe the government is sincere in the fight against corruption. For many agents fighting corruption is very sincere within their agencies and the government as a whole. Those agents told us why many persons do not denounce corruption. The principal reasons invoked are the fear of retaliation and the feeling that the complaints are not considered and that the decisions are not applied. Many agents do not know where to grumble and think that even if a complaint was deposited, there will have no follow up. Certain groups have confided to us that the process is too complex and take time, away to suggest that the simplification of procedures could lead to an increase of denunciations of corruption.

What is the cost of corruption?

According to the latest published data, the disposable income of 60 Haitians over 100 is $ 2 per day. Corruption is a complex phenomenon and it is almost impossible to have an exact idea of the amount of dollars diverted into the channels of mafia crooks of all kinds. However, we can make assumptions based on hypothetical numbers. Ten million dollars embezzled represent a daily failure of $ 2 for 5 million Haitians. In addition, the 60% of Haitians languishing in poverty with their $ 2 a day missed the opportunity to double their disposable income to $ 4. On the other hand, when money for the construction of infrastructures such as bridges, roads, dams, power ports and airports are stolen, the shortfall for the national economy are invaluable. The multiplier effect of such investments is enormous for a small economy such as ours. The most absurd in that phenomenon is that we will repay the money borrowed with interests. I share the patriotic and nationalistic feelings of my old prof. Camille Charlmers when he accuses, condemns with a vociferous tone the negative consequences of the debt of the independence on our backwardness. However, we would like to mention the effects of corruption on our economy are more destructive than the debt of independence honorably paid since the Government of Elie Lescot. In most of models of past and present developments we have analyzed a five-year plan (five consecutive years) is the minimum to boost the economy of a country. At the end of the fifth year, the outcomes of the proposed measures can be tested and proven effectiveness or deficient. In the case of a weak state like Haiti, which is declining in full swing, the negative effects of frauds hamper any attempt to progress this country

CONCLUSIVE REMARK ON CORRUPTION.

That summary underlines the principal observations of our inquiry and suggests the domains and sectors where reforms on governance and against corruption must be in place.

- The high cost of basic services and the cost of life are at the height of national preoccupation in Haiti. Corruption is considered as a serious problem and private firms have précised that is an obstacle important to economic growth.

- The people consider that the bribes are the form of corruption most widespread in Haiti. The users affirm that at the motor vehicle and at customs office more often they have to pay money for the services.

In the public sector, agents estimate that the way of recruiting the staff and the budget decision are relatively complicated. However, the insufficiency of control on budget spending makes it easy for spectacular and illicit fortune of some public employees. The mistrust in the justice system and the police force has leaded the majority of victims to look for other mean of security. The citizens affirm that the Police cannot assume their security. Moreover, many say that international intervention is necessary to help Haiti solve its security problems. The citizens wish to attack the problem of corruption and should be disposed to collaborate in the hard work to eliminate corruption. They think that the Medias, religious institutions and the unit fighting against corruption (ULCC) lead a good battle. However, a vast majority of persons expressed serious reserves concerning the sincerity of government efforts

CHAPTER V

Economic Growth and Poverty in Haiti.

B y definition, poverty is the impossibility by a citizen to satisfy its primary needs. The lack of money increase considerably inequalities of opportunities regarding access to resources such as credit and education. The value system, the weakness of basic social services, the bad conditions of residency, the inability to participate in the public decisions, the lack of social contacts for the poorest are factors that feed poverty. It is the result also of public economy, which has the power of repartition and dispatch enhancement and subvention of resources. For more than two centuries, the economic organization of Haiti has been centered on the advantages of an oligarchy. The misery is fundamentally linked to the lack of access of some assets, principally education; job, capital, credit, social capital, basic services. Education has been more profitable in urban area than rural. That sends to the differences in the conditions and opportunities of putting in value the capacity, especially infrastructures available, markets, credit access. The analysis of the situation regarding the main factors: job, Education, capital, infrastructures (electricity, communications, water) confirms the idea that the causes of poverty fundamentally reside in the lack of assets and unequal repartition of wealth in the country.

The increase of poverty is linked to the bad policies that accompanied the decline of the Haitian economy. The exhaustion of politics, their insufficiencies are also at issue. The neoliberal policy of structural adjustments started in the 1980s has not sufficiently taken the measure of the effects on the separation and natural constraints of the economy. The liberalization and deregulation policy put in place has not been followed of any initiative in matter of reinforcement of the economic capacity of the country. They must aim the decrease of both money and human poverty. We think with a rate of 7 to 8% year over a period of 10 to 15 years, the country will be able to get out of that poverty trap. In addition, a decreasing birth rate up to two or three children per family will help with the demographic problem, cause of that degrading poverty.

The macro-economy can be reoriented to become more motivating in the economic sectors where potentialities will be easily exploited such as agriculture, agro-industry, tourism and the manufacturing sub contracts. In this way, the Central Bank of Haiti should modify its policy of targeting only inflation. It would have to plan a strategy of economic development aiming at jobs creation. In order to favor a fast improvement of output productivity, factor important of competitivety in this world of globalization, some specific sectoriel policy will target the development of appropriate services and contributing to the elaboration of a renovated business environment. The movement of renovation of the basics infrastructure will go on with pre water and cleaning of the street. The Haitian state will pursue its effort of modernization of the educative system aiming at furnishing more accessible services and better quality to the whole population, especially the weakest. Taking into account the difficulty of obtaining large amount of savings and investments in a limited horizon while the pressure is important (for example, the need to create many employments meanwhile the international concurrence becomes more and heavier). One of the strategies to create markets that will be the base for a new Haitian economy will consist to develop many points of growth around specific areas. Those poles could constitute a powerful instrument of growth acceleration in Haiti.

The Economic boom of Dumarsais Estime.

The government of Dumarsais Estime exploited the favorable course of the Economy after the end of World War II to make timely reforms in the country. Despite the hostility of the Dominican caudillo Rafael Trujillo and having managed to calm the concerns of the United States of America, the government began reforms. It encouraged the emergence of a national group of companies, he promoted new legislation to provide social security and the protection of workers, the lawmakers had been able to vote on minimum wage, he developed tourism by funding the construction of hotels and organizing the international exhibition of the bicentenary of Port au Prince. He stimulated the establishment of new industries using foreign investments and local capital. Encouraged by the Ministry of Foreign Affairs, many young Haitians have received scholarships to go abroad to study. The Government launched many economic development projects, social and cultural. The loan of 1922 received from the U.S. government and that devoted the fixed parity of the gourde against the dollar was liquidated and the National Bank passed under Haitian management.

The Economic boom of Paul Magloire.

After the coup of May 10, 1950, social order and peace of the streets have been reinstated. The Economic growth started under the government of Estime continued under Magloire. Provisions to encourage investment in tourism have been taken by the department concerned. On the international market, new openings for our exports had been found. In terms of public works, a modern transportation has been initiated and many streets paving were done through the capital. Thanks to the increased financial participation of the public sector, significant progress was registered in the fields of education and health. According to the Economic Centre for Latin America (CEPAL), the liberalism of President Magloire produced a general economic boom in Haiti. The most striking art of Magloire was to capture all aspects of life easier or making foreign companies liable because they enjoyed great power as long as they shared the profits. Economic growth had slowed, and to make matters worse, Hurricane Hazel devastated the country. Government officials on behalf of their plantations have embezzled the assistance funds received to support because of rampant corruption. Dissatisfaction has won all the population in the absence of immediate solution to the country problems.

The economic stagnation of Francois Duvalier.

The institutions created by Estime and Magloire have enabled the country to benefit from sustained economic growth built on from 1946 to 1955. On arrival of the Duvalier government, no serious economic measure was considered. Too busy to fight his political opponents, Duvalier has seemed to relegate economic problems to the background. Many serious and competent officials were dismissed and replaced by other closed associates of the government macoute. Funds from many financial institutions were diverted to political activities of the regime.

In the private sector, reputed to be very near the former candidate Louis Dejoie, many companies were forced to close because the executive, persecuted, chose exile to avoid wickedness of the new government. In other cases, unfair competition conducted by businesspersons close to the regime has forced other to bankruptcy.

In 1959, the main economic indicators began to fall. According to the data from ECLAC, the Haitian GDP decline from 4.8% to 2.5% in 1961. The annual rate of population grew by 2.5% during the same period. Imports were down 25 percentage in 1959 as well as exports. Clearly, the regime of Francois Duvalier lacked dynamism and force to advance economic growth by strengthening infrastructure. The depletion of our reserves in the National Bank and the balance of payments problems were relieved only by agreement of the International Monetary Fund standby. Surcharge on import and export administered by the macoute regime escalated the country's economic situation in a period of contraction. Revenues from tourism have dramatically diminished and thousands of jobs lost in this sector have exacerbated the already high unemployment in Haiti. As a result, the number of cane cutters, officials and illegal crossing the Haitian Dominican border had increased substantially.

WHAT GROWTH MODEL FOR HAITI?

For many economists without the application of growth theory well articulated, no reduction possible of poverty is possible. The formulation of those theories must allow identifying the causes of the economic stagnation in some regions of the country for decades. First, a good theory of growth must aim at the macroeconomic stability. It must allow the interactions between supply and demand, savings and aggregate demand and finally taking into account the way accumulation of wealth has been done historically.

After the glory days with Dumarsais Estime followed by the one of relatively abundance with Paul Magloire, the economic growth went on a decreasing slope during the Duvalier's years. The economic revolution "Jean claudiste "produced a period of growth but inequalities persisted and the corruption prevented a real repartition of public spending. We had to wait until the beginning of the 80s to see the IMF applies its policy of "structural adjustment "to obtain a durable economic growth. Before the IMF, the Canadian agency of development had tried a strategy called "regional integrated development". That strategy based on the creation of growth pole consisted in the opening of many small projects able to generate revenues in a principal area with the multiplier effect on the neighborhoods. The Canadians thought that the persisting economic stagnation in those areas could be transformed in growth only by a flow of investments directed toward the most affected zones. Unfortunately, that approach failed and the Canadian advisers left the country empty-handed. The causes of that failure resided in the corruption and inefficacity of the Haitian public administration. Today with new growth theories, Haitian economists should be able to create others alternate plans for a durable economic growth. Let us mention three ideas to obtain endogenous mean of progress.

A) The State should be able to create an economic environment favorable to investors.

B) A class of managers willing to invest must stand out.

C) The utilization of new technologies and new procedures in all sector of the production process.

Let us remind that since 200 years, Haiti is looking for a political stability. From 1915 to 1934, during the first US occupation, Haiti enjoyed a prolonged period of relative stability. The situation held up after the departure of the occupants in 1934. Presidents were elected democratically. The Americans created a new public administration. A new army under hierarchy was trained and installed by the marines. In spite of all, Haiti did not enjoy prosperity at that time. The main reason was the absence of capital to engage activities of development. The occupants preferred to terminate the loan to Parish. After they left in 1934, signs of economic development were not too many in Haiti. Dumarsais Estime, the president elected after the anti Lescot process represents in Haitian history one of the most progresssistes. He realized some important public works in the country, which opened the way for economic growth. In addition, the position of his government regarding social demands allowed him to conquer the heart of a vast majority of Haitians. The economic environment created by Dumarsais Estime generated a multiplier that a bourgeoisie could exploit to the start up of Haiti. Unfortunately, the General Paul E Magloire stopping the good climate for investments established by Estime toppled him. The military regime of Paul Magloire and the dictatorship of Duvalier (father & son) could not maintain the economic growth initiated by Estime.

Nowadays, the improvement of factors leading to an increase of the national production is the condition to get the country out of poverty. How to generate a durable economic growth in Haiti? I think that the pitiful situation of Haiti today necessitates some overhaul in the system. The excessive centralization of the Haitian political and administrative system represents one of the necessary conditions to push the country forward. New growth theories focus now on:

a) The liberalization of commerce with the lowering of customs tariffs from 50% to 90% on certain products.
b) Deregulation in order to facilitate the procedures of starting up new firms and the manufacturing of new products.
c) Deep reform of the tax code in Haiti. For example, one could reduce the marginal tax rate on some type of investments.
d) An increase of foreign direct investments. (In the Haitian case, in spite of the good will of the Diaspora to invest in Haiti, welcome structures have never been put in place. Corruption and the time lag to start a business in the country slow down the amount of investments the country could benefit from Haitian living abroad. For historical reasons, Haiti cannot attire the influx of financial capital generated by the World international. The bad image of the country maintained constantly by foreign medias push back tourists and investors)

Is the application of the new growth theories enough to launch the Haitian economy? Economists from World Bank and the IMF already advised most of those theories. In 1996, the Finance minister of Rene Preval had declared :<< I applied the neoliberal policy in Haiti >>. However, he did not mention a word concerning the results obtained. Many public firms were privatized. A new investments code was written. Nevertheless, when Jean Bertrand Aristide succeeded to Preval in 2000, a technical evaluation of that theory was not realized.

POVERTY REDUCTION VS ECONOMIC DEVELOPMENT.

I think that economic growth can be defined as the arithmetic increase of the national production over a fiscal period. For some economists, economic growth goes further; they have to include the increase of the ability to produce, the improvement of the technological facility and ideological adjustments for an economy to grow. Whatever the definition adopted, economic growth should be the means and economic development the end in order to augment the national wealth. The term "economic development "goes farther than an arithmetic increase of the national revenue. It includes the general improvement of life conditions in the nation. One must insert the social progress in the life of the citizens. It necessitates a change in the structure of distribution of national revenue based on demographic trends occurred in the country.

After an observation and analysis of the economic measures adopted in the country for the last 20 years, I draw the conclusion that we are not going in the right direction. Haitian economists at the Central Bank maintain a policy of macroeconomic stability to allow growth. However, can they grow production with interests averaging 25 to 30%? As recommended by the IMF, all Haitian governments have reduced spending; privatize public firms in order to reduce the budget deficit. Like in 1986 after the departure of Jean Claude Duvalier, customs reform continued until 1994 after the return of Aristide to power. Following the massive liberalization of commerce and deregulation of public firms, the Haitian State does not dispose money to make public investments. Follow our reasoning:

a) The Central Bank applies a contractionary policy

b) The chronic budget deficit prevent the State to invest

Almost 90% of the national budget is devoted to payroll. The international donations and the remittances of the Diaspora represent the only way of survival for a vast majority of Haitians. Many economists call such situation: poverty trapped.

THE NEOLIBERALISM IN HAITI.

Marc Bazin (1981-1982).

After the fasts of the presidential weddings, Marc Bazin became Finance Ministry of Jean Claude Duvalier. After a tour of the World leading him to the Middle East in search of loans for the government, Emmanuel Bros Finance Ministry at that time came back empty handed. The need of liquidity by the Jean Claude Duvalier regime, forced them to accept the World Bank's handpicked, Marc Bazin, alias Mr. Clean to reform Haiti finances. Energetically, he accomplished his duties. He reduced the customs franchise enjoyed by the "macoute "in order to increase gross receipts. Then, he attacked the non-budgeted accounts where the government spent freely. Specially, the "Regie du Tabac et des allumettes "where excise taxes were not counted in the national budget. For the first time in Haiti, a minister has spoken to the media about the financial situation of the country. He invited all agents to tighten their belts so that the budget deficit could be reduced. In the streets, the US dollars became suddenly rare. Since the 1912 convention, dedicating fix parity between the Haitian Gourde and the US dollars, for the first time Haitians who needed the green back had to buy them at a very low rate in the Streets. The association of Bazin with the Duvalier's was very short. Panicked by financial decisions of the minister to fight fiscal evasion, the macoutes went to complaint to their boss. For example, the order installed at the Regie du tabac et des allumettes gave problems to some executives of the regime. Some close associates of the President felt the suppression of unjustified spending by the Bazin staff badly. Certain extremist macoutes talked about a plot to put the regime in difficulty. After a few months, Jean Claude Duvalier fired Bazin or Mr. Clean and the same day he embarked to the USA via Santo Domingo. A festive atmosphere saluted the departure of Mr. Clean from the Duvalier's administration. The zealous fans of Duvalier had not realized that the mission of Marc Bazin if succeeded could have saved their regime. The survival of the regime for life depended on the success of Mr. Clean. They will regret it in the following years.

USAID (1983-1986)

After Marc Bazin failure, the international organization had not given up on Haiti. Experts from Washington joining with USAID put up a new plan for Haiti. They proposed to reorient a part of the Haitian agriculture toward exportations. In compensation, they should encourage the increase of assembly industry in the country. Up to that point, Haiti was able to nourish his population. The outcome of the new economic approach was immediately felt. The agriculture productivity declined meanwhile the demography kept on increasing. Food importations passed from 62 to 89 million since 1983 to 1987, representing an average of 20% the country total importations. The "Food for works" and the "Food for peace "program, two NGOs, started the importation of food and cereal products for distribution to the poor. Even the free distribution of food products could not satisfy the market need. Threatened by hunger, peasants moved toward Port au Prince. From 720.000 inhabitants in 1980, the population of Port au Prince grew to 1 million in 1986. That was the beginning of the construction of shantytowns surrounding the capital. Cap Haitian inhabitants augmented from 50.000 in 1980 to 80.000 in 1986.The internal movement followed migration where many young Haitians left Port-au Prince, which became saturated, toward countries like the USA, Canada, and Venezuela. A well- known Haitian journalist called that trend dpm kante (straight to Miami). Our exportations increased because of the assembly industries grouped in the industrial park closed to the Airport. Around 60.000 jobs were generated by those factories. On a fiscal point of view, the poor entries were insignificant because of the low salary paid to the workers. Most of those plants benefited of the exemption right to export. In fact, it constituted a strategy used by the commerce ministry to attire them.

That plan was the last attempt by the USAID to salvage the Duvalier regime. The kleptomania of some supporter of that regime had a bad impact on the Haitian economy. Instead of improving, the country declined. The economic growth started in the middle of the 70s could not stand pace with the increasing population. The lack of investments in education resulted in a less qualified workforce. As that happened in some Asians countries, the assembly sector could not transform to an industrial sector. The educative system has been abandoned to private and religious schools. In the rural area, the case was worst because the ratio of teacher/student stayed at one for 60. Our imports kept increasing until to represent twice of our exports. In 1985, the budget deficit attained 160 millions USD. The remittances of the Diaspora allowed to maintaining a certain quantity of foreign reserves, which protected the Gourde. From 1981 to 1986, foreign journalists affirm that Jean Claude Duvalier had embezzled the equivalent of half the Haitian budget. In 1984, hunger riots broke in Gonaives. The ministries sent to calm down the population were received by stones and protests. The presence of macoutes in the town had not made fear of anything. Used to political turmoil, the Haitians started a fight against the heir of Duvalier's. In the meantime, the Bennett's under the control of the president godfather had occupied a large political spot in the country.

The choc provoked by the fight among many factions of the dictatorship started shaking the duvalierism wall. The referendum organized by Roger Lafontant had confirmed the loss of popular support to the regime. As always and since 1915, the eyes of Washington were scrutinizing what is going on in the house of their small troubling neighbor and, they planned the transition to Jean Claude Duvalier. The departure of Jean Claude Duvalier announced by Larry Speaks on January 30, 1986 was in reality the last ultimatum issued by the Reagan Administration to Baby doc. The expressions of joy from the Diaspora in the Friday morning were the proof to the World that Haitians needed the departure of Duvalier. The arrests and persecutions enticed by the macoutes will go on until the dawn of February 7, 2007; they were the cause of the violence against them by the population after the official announcement by Duvalier himself that he was stepping down.

1986-1987: Leslie Delatour

The national council headed by Henry Namphy named Leslie Delatour as the Finance ministry. They said he was picked by Washington which imposed the choice to the national council of government. Upon his installation, he will start reforming the Haitian economy. The model of structural adjustment implemented by the Funds everywhere in the Third World, refused by the Duvalierists with the firing of Marc Bazin in 1981, was going to be adopted plainly. One can say that Leslie Delatour revised the USAID plan we mentioned earlier in this book.

A) Maintain without interruption an annual growth of 4.5%

B) Limit increase in prices in Haiti or avoid importing inflation abroad.

C) Realize during the period 1986-1987, and after, every year and during two years, a budget surplus of 1.5% of the PIB. (p201, Kawas Francois, La crise de l'Etat en Haïti de 1986 a 1990).

At first, the new ministry attacked the corrupt methods of Duvalier's. The monopolies accorded to the State enterprises were revoked. The reduction of spending of the government was realized. A review of the custom code lowered tariffs on some products. In order to compensate the reduction in the entries, the US government increased its aid from 54 to 180 million USD. A pack of measures was put in place to assume the economic revival in the aftermath of Duvalier's. Let us cite for example: the closing of the sugar plants of Darbonne (Leogane) and Welsh (Limomade), the Bon Repos Hospital, the Bank of credit to Agriculture (BCA), and the National Bank of credit to agriculture and industry (BNDAI).

The national council of government (CNG) with Leslie Delatour continued with the policy of zero tax to export in order to encourage the implantations of new subcontract industries in the country. The government wanted to increase the energy capacity and the improvement of the telecommunication system in the country. The national council of government gave the warranty to investors to maintain order in the Union. The ministry Delatour claimed at high voice: the assembly industries allow the creation of jobs, which Haiti needs badly. However, the union movement was well established and answered to workers complaint when necessary. In countries where that type of industries are functioning the docility of workers are very important. For example, on the arrival of the first subcontract industries in the 1970s, the minimum wage was about one dollar a day. Through the end of 1986, some workers won up to five dollars /day. An increasing inflation at about 20% during the same period reduced the purchasing power of the workers. We need also to mention the lack of formation of our unionized workers and the inherent tendency of Haitians to revolt. Under the effect of those factors, in the year 1987 14.000 jobs left Haiti to other countries specially the Dominican Republic.

The tenure of Leslie Delatour as finance ministry was very short. However, its economic reform was felt as a small revolution. His arrogance and his manner put oil in the fire. Leftist's politicians attacked him continuously and transformed his image as an American agent in Haiti. In reality, Delatour with his strategy of laissez faire did not prove clearly his economic plan. He gave no explanation to explain the closing of the national enterprises of vegetables (ENAOL), and the sugar plant of Darbonne. In a country where public health is so inefficient, no reason was giving for the shutdown of the hospital center of Bon Repos. No study was realized to justify the need of closing of the enterprises. He closed his eyes on the struggling, which invaded the Haitian markets and the loss of revenue for the Haitian tax department. He ignored the effect of contraband on the local production and the discouraged Haitian peasants planted only to satisfy their personnel needs. He devoted an increase of 11% in the Education Budget but the literacy campaign organized by the Catholic Church should have been subsidized.

The hopes of an economic take off born after the end of the Duvalier has scaled down. The attempt of neoliberal's reform with the installation of a Chicago Boy at the office of Finance gave no spectacular results. In the short term, the lowering of prices benefited to the consumers, but in the midterm, the jobs lost could never came back and when we know that in Haiti a job is a luxury product, one can guess easily the image transferred to the posterity by Leslie Delatour.

FEBRUARY 7, 1991- SEPTEMBER 30, 1991
LEFTIST GOVERNMENT AND RIGHTIST ECONOMIC POLICY

Once installed in the National Palace, Jean Bertrand Aristide realized that leading a country is different from political activism. The first measures of the government went in the direction inverse of the traditional anti capitalist sermon of the old priest. The government accepted the reduction of public employees by 8000. Drastic measures were put in place at the tax department and in a short period a large amount of money was collected. From February to June 1991, monthly spending of the government lowered from 32.9 million to 17 million USD. The IMF waited for the government at the corner and after hesitations, functionaries of the regime sat down at the table of negotiation. A standby agreement was signed according loans up to 500 millionsUSD.

1994: The failure of Smark Michel

The operations "return to Democracy "organized by the Clinton administration to reinstate Aristide to power allowed the destitute Haitian president to end his term. The Americans have controlled the operation from start to end. The toppling of Cedras appeared a just cause for the Haitian population and the rest of the World. However, the former Saint Jean Bosco priest, a well-known anti capitalist proponent. He used to call that ideology a mortal sin, however he had to living now with it inside his house.

They were whispering in some Washington area that he has signed a pack of secret conditions with Washington in order to make possible his comeback. The coexistence of a populist president with a government applying the neoliberals' agenda could not last for long. The paradigms and the revolutionary slogan will bend eventually in front of the market realty. Following the installation of Smark Michel and the publication of his program, the wall of Lavalas started cracking. The privatization of State Enterprises, main source of entries for Haiti government, was put ahead of priorities by the International Monetary Funds. Furthermore, the program of structural adjustment asked for a reduction of subvention and spending of the State. Aristide and Preval were scared that those decisions affected their popularity. Many populist organizations closed to the power organized streets protests against the privatization of the State run enterprises. Jean Bertrand Aristide and the persons in his staff did not take any steps to restore order. The white were not dupe. They insisted on the respects of the papers signed at Washington by Aristide for his return to power. Some well-informed sources have given tips on those papers:

Maintain a climate of democratic Dialogue with all political sector of the country.

Pay the arrears owed to the IMF to facilitate more loans.

NGOs will install new projects in the country.

A monetary policy to fight inflation

Privatization of State runs enterprises (Starting with TELECO)

As it happened in earlier years with the FNCD of Turnep Delpe and K plim after the 1990 election, Titid wanted to get rid of the legal hat borrowed in Washington. After months, the government was turning around and losing time. Aristide wanted to negotiate the remaining of his term instead of the economic program in Washington. Stocked between the anvil and the hammer, the Prime Minister Smark Michel resigned. The Americans closed the way and as always, the other donor's countries take the same direction with them.

DEMOGRAPHY AND ECONOMIC GROWTH.

The old macro economic theories have always considered the increase in population as an important factor for economic growth. Rhetoricians did not take time to search on the origins of economic growth but instead on the means to reinforce it. Alfred Malthus, one of the great economists of the 19th century predicted the bad effect of a population increase on growth. Based on his model, to avoid misery a country economic growth should augment at an average superior to population increase.

In the Haitian case, until the middle of the twenty first century, equilibrium allowed the country to avoid the deep poverty. In thirty years, the Haitian population increased at a pace of 2% meanwhile the economy grew with an average varying from 1 to 4%. Some political events like the September 30, 1991 coup sanctioned by a three-year embargo have diminished the national production by 25%. When the international community reestablished institutional order in the country, solutions to fill in the deficit gap of 3 years were not envisaged. Instead, a political conflict leads to a suspension of the international aid. In the meantime, the population kept increasing, putting pressure on the few resources of the country. Certain economists advocate a policy of reduction of the population. In the 80s, the diffusion of National televised programs to discourage the number of non-desired pregnancies gave substantial results. I think that the responsible nowadays must return with those old policies aiming at the reduction of births.

What is the nature of the labor market in Haiti?

Since the opening of the industrial park during the government of Jean Claude Duvalier nearly 50,000 jobs were created over a period of five to six years, nothing like this had happened in Haiti. Curiously, we could not find any program of massive job creation in the political parties so hungry for power in the country. The sous traitance industry lost ground after the departure of Jean-Claude Duvalier in Haiti. Political unrests have forced factories to be relocated in the Dominican Republic and Central America. The tourism sector plunged in agony after accusation against of AIDS was launched by the CDC against us in the early 80s. Despite the creation of banks to finance housing in Haiti, the construction sector has not been booming. The absence of reliable credit policy for the middle class may explain the nonchalance observed in this area. We believe that the bankers of the housing sector were afraid to take too many risks because of political turpitude in Haiti. Agriculture accounts for about half of the employment market in the country. After that comes in second the informal sector as another important source of employment. Supplied through smuggling, this sector is a sort of refuge for thousands of landless peasants fleeing our provinces. We were able to detect the absence of official statistics on employment in Haiti. We hope that the Haitian Institute of Statistics and Informatics establish regional offices to periodically record employment in the country.

In a development perspective, the Haitian education system is not ready to produce the necessary frameworks. Do not forget that economic growth is positively correlated with the level of education. A visit to some schools in Port au Prince establishes the difference: some of them have data centers while other students have not yet had the chance to touch a computer. At the time of the American occupation, when inequality to attend school had been reduced, a middle class of doctors, nurses, engineers and other technicians in many other areas was created. We suggest that future leaders of the country to think about basic education first. A true educational reform should start at primary level. In the nine departments of the country new schools should be built and education to the end of primary education should be free. The improvement of the curriculum at the secondary level should be considered. The Haitian system is too theoretical and contains too many unnecessary classes. We need to introduce the system of elective classes in the Haitian system to enable our students to have more choices.

Today many Haitian professionals reside abroad, which is proof of the country's inability to maintain our graduates. We have nothing against the University. But education reform in Haiti must start at the primary level. It is sad to see them go meeting the requirements of other countries. When subcontracting factories installed in Haiti in the 80s needed skilled technicians, they had to go to Panama, Mexico or the Dominican Republic. During the same period our universities poured on the local market with writers, lawyers, diplomats, managers. The Haitian private sector must invest in the training of modernization because the Haitian education system will benefit them in the medium term. Unfortunately in small countries such as Haiti, the industry often fails to fulfill its role. The State is obliged to take care of almost all social functions.

A GROWTH MODEL POST JANUARY 12, 2010

Invest simultaneously in all three sectors starting with the primary.

In the numerous books written on Haiti, which we had the chance to read, and the search we led on the field, we realized that the authors tend to approach the Haitian economy on two aspects: the agricultural sector and the non-agricultural sector. It is a fact that agriculture now is the sector with the most jobs in Haiti. Many economists and numerous international institutions realize that the increase in agricultural productivity still represents a first step toward economic development. In the conjuncture of after January 12, 2010, we want to offer a theoretical model of durable economic growth. According to Jeffrey Sachs, the best mean to solve chronic poverties in many countries is the use of bottom up growth model. The lack of available data for some variable such as the amount of the international aid and the leak caused by corruption in Haiti, we simply created a linear model. We think that the conjuncture post January 12 necessitates such plan. We abandon the design of the operational plan to the cadre of the Haitian public administration.

Court Term

Let us assume that political stability is back with the election of a President and a Congress, and the natural disasters avoid Haiti.

Let us assume that the donor's countries and the international organizations respect their engagement toward Haiti. We envisage using the aid in order to produce a choc simultaneous in all economic sectors.

Primary sector:

Reform the agriculture with goal to increase the productivity that is to say the yield by Hectare. Launch a program of reforestation and soil protection (green revolution). The under sectors such as fishing, aviculture, livestock must be taken into account in the modernization.

Secondary sector:

Negotiate with the Americans the application of the Hope laws. Open a third industrial park in the center department. The mining department should go on with the prospection for oil and other metal.

Tertiary sector:

Rebuild all the public offices destroyed during the earthquake. The collection of tons of scraps abandoned on the ground, the realization of a land plan for the country. Make credit more accessible to public and private sector employees wishing to reconstruct their houses. Priority will be given to those willing to rebuild destroyed Schools.

Medium term
Primary sector

Many workers will be out of jobs after the first round augmentation of the agriculture productivity. That surplus of workers should be directed toward the other two sectors of the economy.

Secondary Sector

Decentralization should allow the creation of at least three industrial areas able to absorb a part of underemployed from the farm.

Tertiary Sector

That sector should substitute the primary as the main source of jobs. The rebuilding work started in the short term should go on principally with the construction of new roads aiming at the unblocking of the country, favoring the take off in local tourism. A reform of the educative system allowing the eradication of illiteracy.

Long term
Primary Sector

The reform in education started in the short term should allow the agrarian sector to keep contact with modern agriculture. Even if the country has not attended food self-sufficiency, a decrease in food importations should occurred, allowing to the central Bank to retain that flood of currency leaving the country. Economic data from of the last years have proved that augmentation of price in petroleum products and food consumptions represent a constant threat for economic growth. The current account deficit will reduce and the gourde will stay more stable.

Secondary Sector

Educative reforms initiated in the short term should allow us to begin at least a second phase of industrialization. Exploitation of mines of gold, nickel should allow the Haitian State to solve its dependency problem from international charity.

Tertiary Sector

In that sector, the future belongs to tourism (local & international). The modernization of touristic possibilities initiated in the midterm should accelerate and allow us to attain the level of our Caribbean neighbors.

MATHEMATIC FORM OF OUR SECTORIEL MODEL

C = Economic Growth
S1= Primary Sector
S2= Secondary sector
S3= Tertiary Sector
Court Term= 1-2 years
Mid Term= 2-5 years
Long Term= 5 years+
U= A constant representing the primary sector in the long-term economic development.

K= A constant representing political stability, international aid and natural disaster

L= A constant representing time lag.

We have our function like this:

Court Term:

C= [KL (s1+s2+s3)] (1)

Let us assume that our equation remains unchanged in the short term. In the long term, our growth function becomes:

Long Term:

C= {S1+[KL (S2+S3)]} (2)

CHAPTER VI

Case for a new approach in Budget allocation

A transparency management of the budget is a key sign of good governance. We have talked with some public employee on the decision process and the managerial method used inside their respective departments. In most cases, the results confirm the trend of what is said in the general public.

We try to understand the level of coordination between the Finance Ministry and the other agencies. The employee told us that the Finance Ministry worked closely with agencies in the preparation of the Budget. Some key employee working in the preparation of the Budget agrees that all the process leading to the final version of the Budget is well coordinated. In agreement with the elected officials, the Budget of communes is prepared under the supervision of employee of the Finance ministry.

Meanwhile some employees in other agencies denied knowing anything in the process of the Budget. They affirm that the decisions are not controlled internally in their agencies. That is why in numerous agencies they do not audit internally too often. However, a vast majority of servants confirm that an external audit took place at least every three years because of bad management.

In average, some servants involved in the budget process think that there is mismanagement in the allocation of resources. Political pressures from some well-connected persons always try to influence the Budget. Others mention that some allocations are influenced by briberies.

For the fiscal year 2010-2011, the budget has displayed spending of 108 billions of gourdes, which is a record according to the ministry. However, they did not mention that the Haitian treasury would disburse only 29 milliards of the 108. Every year Haiti receives donation from other countries to support its budget. When a surprised event such as hurricane happens, the government does not have any mean to intervene. They have to go out begging for donations everywhere. In order to maintain the stability required by the International monetary funds, the Central Bank of Haiti cannot emit new paper money. The Central Bank is working under the watch of International monetary funds. We used the 2009-2010 Budget as model to suggest some modification in the budget allocation. We found that some expenses are non-productive. They could spend them in other sector that we think need priority.

We did an investigation through Port-au-Prince and we realized that the country needs a new land plan. The constructions of the last 25 years do not pay property taxes to the department of taxes. In the table of current receipts, we realized that property taxes represent only 0.94% of the total entries. We suggest also the payment of tolls in the entrance or exit of the nine departments. These taxes could help maintain the roads.

Budget Deficit

The budget deficits are one of the first factors of economic instability. The immediate consequence is an increase of the inflation rate, disequilibrium in the current account, and the exit of capital. The last time Haiti had a budget surplus was in 1968. Generally, Haitian governments finance the deficit by loaning money from the Central Bank leaving a long list of arrears. The excess of printing money leads to increase in inflation because the money created does not correspond to a GDP increase. As a result, inflation augmented exponentially in Haiti during the last 30 years. The lost of purchasing power is so depth that the middle class tend to flee the country.

Management of contract offer

The way the public administration manages the contract offer is a very important mean of efficiency and transparency. Information obtained from public employee reveals that the rules in the way contracts are obtained are not clear. Less than half of employee thought the rules of contract offers are well written. However, a vast majority of employee are agreeing to tell that the process of contract offer is too centralized.

In spite of the confusion in the attribution of contracts many employees will tell you, there was no fraud in the process. A few employees are agreeing they are briberies in the process. We have been told that rate of payment for the bribes varied from 0.9 to 10% of the amount of the contract. Furthermore, the contracts accepted were those of the foreign companies. I suggest in the future that the Planning Ministry will direct the process in the countryside where the work will be done.

REFORM OF THE PUBLIC SECTOR IN HAITI

The public administration in Haiti is a cause of our lateness and the poverty in the country. Historically, agents of the public administration must submit to the actual regime. In spite the opening of new schools to prepare the agents, no serious changed occurred. A good civil service is vital for the accomplishments of economic growth. The result of the public sector regarding quality of services will influence the procedure to manage the agents. The budget must be distributed according to the needs and priorities of the country. The recruitment policy, advancement, and supervision are key factors for a good management of all public sectors. The lack of respects for the procedure facilitates the way for corruption. In Haiti, the failure to accomplish good results has encouraged our donators to use nongovernmental organization (NGO) to avoid our public administration. Some aid agencies question the competency of their Haitian partners. I had the chance to read a document regarding the period of time to open a business in the Caribbean, Haiti was classified as the country where it takes longer to do so. The paper proved that the required documents to open a business in Haiti could stay for months in the drawer of the commerce ministry. The reduction of poverty is linked to a performing public sector. The access to quality services is a key element in the improvement of the poor life. Corruption has always existed in Haiti, but today it is exaggerated in proportion. Public agent's credibility is so low that the public does not trust them. Let us remark that the institutions were money is not involved represent the more respected by the population. For example, institutions such as economic and statistics department, governmental media have a good reputation among the users. Although, inside some of those institutions exist a phenomenon called "check zombies "which consist to have more employee on the payroll list than the real number of working persons. The political dependency of some agencies to others prevents managers to follow the norms. Under the Duvalier regime, only macoutes had the right to be part of the civil service. During the Lavalass period, being a victim of the old Duvalier regime constituted a solid reference to obtain a job in the Haitian public sector. Moreover, the Lavalas government required militancy and capacity to gather people for public manifestation when needed.

In many public agencies, a salary scale does not exist or when there is one policy maker rarely looks at it to give increase. That is why many agents are trying to hold two jobs. In some countries, it is prohibited to do that. Moreover, nepotism must be eliminated in the Haitian public administration because it affects the employee performance level. The importance of the public sector is growing and it remains the principal employer in Haiti. The private sector in Haiti is still underdeveloped to satisfy the country needs. Therefore, the Haitian Public Administration has to play a crucial role in the improvement of the poverty.

SUGGESTION TO INCREASE GOVERNMENT GROSS RECEIPTS IN HAITI.

I read a lot economic plans after the January 12, 2010 earthquake; numerous of them do not focus on the financial aspect, which I think represent one of the key problems in the Haitian poverty. Beside of a plan by sector published in another chapter of that book, we have decided to submit a model to increase the revenue of the government. The inability of Haiti to repay its debt prevents the use of a financial tool like bonds to raise money. In the 1960s, Francois Duvalier government failed to pay the bonds issued at that time called for "The national renovation". Some economists ask for the creation of a "reconstruction Bank ", but they do not give information where the capital will come from. Many countries, which gave charities to Haiti during the New York meeting, have already forgotten about their promises. The political chaos in Haiti constitutes a good pretext to avoid that engagement. We try to indentify the main source of revenue of the Haitian state:

Taxes from the Custom Administration
Taxes from the Contribution department
Donation from foreign governments
Donation from international organizations
Loan with low interest from some foreign governments
Loan with low interest from international organizations
Loan from the Central Bank (money printing)
In the last budget (2010-2011), the rate of international support goes above 60% of our national budget. To survive in the coming years, Haiti will need more source of revenue.

Reform at the Custom Administration

Adjust the custom code so that taxes on some luxury products are increased.

Computerized the system of custom slips to reduce the fraud.

Increase control of the custom offices in provinces in at the border with the Dominican Republic.

Reform at the "Contribution department"

Build a land plan to identify all the new constructions of the last 30 years and tax them.

Zone called Bourgeois must pay more

A uniform lump payment can be fixed for the shantytowns.

Establish a temporary tax at the airport (2 to 5 years) for leaving the country. The BRH must collect those taxes directly and transfer them in a budgeted account.

Establish a toll at the entrance of the two most visited provinces: Cap & Cayes.

Establish a national lottery based on the model of the old lottery peligre, that is to say, tickets are mandatory for public employees and some businesses in the private sector could acquire a quota of tickets.

The office of vehicle insurance could increase temporarily the insurance on luxury vehicle.

PS.

That was already on the publisher house when we learned the new administration of president Martelly is taxing the Diaspora on the remittances and on the phone calls. We are very happy with that initiative. We hope that the new government will allow transparency to help the public to understand the path of that new revenue for the country.

CHAPTER VII

January 12, 2010: free fall to hell.

The town of Port au Prince and his inhabitants were doing businesses as usual in this Tuesday January 12. A kind of political tension reigned through the country because of the electoral fraud organized by Rene Preval to take control of the parliament during the last election. News media just announced the murder in broad day light of a university professor in a street of the capital. Moreover, the students of the National Institute of Administration and Management (INAGHEI) were already in the streets to protest against that slaying. At 4h52 according to some eyewitnesses, everything started shaking. Someone told me that he had closed his eyes during the first choc, when he reopened them; hc saw only cadavers and scraps around him. The dust resulted from the collapse of many buildings covered the sky. The cries of people trapped under the rubbish could be heard from a long distance. The incapacity of poor States like Haiti was being proved. There is no fire department in Port au Prince. The Haitian National Police are not equipped to deal with such situation. By the way, the head quarter of the National police had collapse. The inhabitants of Port au Prince organize themselves to save as many people as they could. Some people showed heroism because they used their hands to lift up heavy walls and stone rubbishes. We have to mention that in Haiti houses are built with concrete. There is no building code in Haiti. Constructions are made based on the wishes of the owners. Before the earthquake, building collapse was usual event in Haiti. The night extended slowly and the spectacle was becoming worst and worst. No way to go around, the city was completely dark, only the lights of some cars were source of vision for the rescuers. No places were available to transport some injured, because many hospitals collapsed. Therefore, some victims were dying quietly assisted by their parents and neighbors.

No sign of the country leaders, even the president Preval who many thought was under the craps inside the National Palace. It was completely dark in the night and a silence of mausoleum glided upon the city. The rescuers now tired went to sleep in the streets waiting for tomorrow.

The social assessment.

About 1 million people, 10% of Haiti population were affected directly or indirectly. The number of dead has been established closed to 225.000. Almost 300.000 were injured. Some 800.000 persons went to live under the tents. The public administration has collapsed. No security exists under the tents. Rapes and sexual abuses occurred every minute. Some 40.000 prisoners evade the central jail of the town without traces. The US Air Forced has saved many lives by taking over the main Airport of Haiti allowing the first aids to arrive.

The economic assessment.

A) Infrastructure.

The damages are considerable. About 200.000 houses were damaged and 105.000 destroyed; 1300 schools at all level and 50 hospitals were destroyed. The Presidential Palace, the justice Palace, the Palace of all ministries, the head quarter of the National Police, a lot of police station have been destroyed. 70 kilometers of paved roads have been damaged and some of them are key ways.

B) Environment

The impact of the disaster will last for long on the Haitian environment. Pollution and outbreak of some diseases will threat Haiti for the coming years. Port au prince is living with 40-cube meter of rubbished through the streets.

C) Industry sector

There is no building code in Haiti, so the houses were not building according to any rule paraseismic. On January 12, we had the result, under the choc some quarter have been destroyed.

d) lost of Jobs

The earthquake of January 12, 2010 caused a huge number of jobs losses in Haiti. Many activities stopped completely. The interruption of financial activities forced many people out of businesses. The informal sector counted the most victims because of the death of many streets merchants operating in the center of Port au Prince. The unemployment rate in Haiti is officially at 65%. Those numbers hide the underemployment in the informal sector and some businesses activities that are making ridiculous profit. There is no office for unemployment in each department of the country and even the Haitian Institute of Statistics relies on projections about the unemployment numbers in the country. In such conditions, 75% is a reasonable number for estimating the unemployment rate in Haiti

FOR A NEW APPROACH IN THE HOUSING POLICY IN HAITI.

The superficies of the Haitian State is 27,749 square kilometers. The last estimates of the Statistic Haitian Institute in 2010 project the Haitian population at 10.040.000 people, which is a density of 362 persons by square kilometers. The topography of the country is build up with 60% of mountains sometimes steep. The cultivable part is very small and has been reducing year after year. Specially, the method of culture is destroying the land. All of these elements worsened the situation where we have to look for new ways to satisfy the housing need of the increasing population.

CONSTRUCTION OF SHELTERS.

The Haitian Housing Department could start building some huge space able to shelter a lot of people temporarily. The space will be provided based on the amount of persons available. For example, some small temporary units should be built in some specific areas around the countryside closed to Port au Prince. Once the economic conditions of those families satisfied, they have to move leaving the space for other person in need.

CONSTRUCTION OF HOUSES FOR WORKING FAMILY.

Housing does not have to be a donation. The exceptional crisis created by the earthquake and the constraints we just wrote about in this chapter, force us to think that the government cannot afford to distribute houses as gifts. In the past most Haitian government, realize such distribution to satisfy their clients. Today the reality is different. They could subsidize housing to working family or they could use some stabilization law to protect low-income family. With the establishment of an income limit rule, some families will be excluded in this program. In addition, the construction of housing should be extended to some provinces. Some countryside like, Leogane, Croix des bouquets, Gressier could have their housing section. Here are some basic ideas that we think could serve the starting point or as reference to the technician of Haiti housing Department.

INTERIM HAITI RECOVERY RECONSTRUCTION

In the aftermath of the violent earthquake that rocked Haiti, the international community regrouped in a meeting at New York decided to create a fund to help rebuild the country. A panel of 60 countries promised about 9 millions dollars. The Haitian parliament gave the legal structure for that entity to function.

The mandate of the Interim Commission for the Reconstruction of Haiti (IHRC) is to provide strategic planning, coordination and implementation of resources from bilateral

In addition, multilateral donors, non-governmental sector business, offering all the necessary transparency and accountability. The IHRC has to work to make the best investments and contributions of these partners.

The IHRC is responsible for the development and ongoing review of development plans for Haiti, assessing the needs and gaps and setting priorities for investments. It approves the project proposals in terms of their consistency and their coordination with the Plan of Action for the Rehabilitation and Development of Haiti (PARDH). Although the Commission is able to develop and apply for projects that fall within the priorities of the Action Plan, they must decide on the reliability and the admissibility of external submissions.

The IHRC conducts its activities under the Act on the state of emergency. Therefore, it has the powers necessary to carry out its activities. It ensures the timely implementation of development projects and priorities, including by facilitating the issuance of title deeds and permits for the construction of hospitals, power generation, ports and other development projects necessary for the economy.

To facilitate the timely implementation and effective priorities and projects approved by the IHRC, the departments concerned will designate members of their staff to work within the IHRC. Given the critical and immediate identification and mobilization of land for relocation of displaced populations, the construction of long-term housing and schools and job creation, the agents appointed for this purpose by the Ministry of Economy and Finance must have the skills necessary to review records and to issue land titles requested by the IHRC within 15 working days.

The IHRC will provide the relevant ministries with the international technical assistance necessary to enable them to strengthen their capacity in order to perform their duties efficiently and quickly on priorities and projects.

We have classified the type of projects the IHRC is trying to invest the funds collected.

1) Building capacity
2) Pick up Garbage
3) Education
4) Energy
5) Health
6) Public housing
7) Jobs
8) Water purification
9) Multisectoriel
10) Others

We have counted 77 projects, which already received the funding necessary: We aligned them by the highest percentage.

Health: 20 projects 26%
Employment: 16 projects 20.7%
Public Housing: 13 projects 16.9%
Miscellaneous: 10 projects 13%
Capacity development: 6 projects 7.8%
Education: 5 projects 6.5%
Energy: 4 projects 5.2%
Garbage Removal: 3 projects 3.9%

The total amount of money voted by the board of IHRC for those projects are 3.151.310.000 dollars representing about 35% of the funds promised in New York.

In our development plan presented previously in that book, we have insisted that all three sectors of the economy are pushed at the same time. In that first round of projects and investments we think that the sector tertiary has benefited of more than 80% of the funds, we have no problems because of the character urgent of projects like pick up garbage, water sanitation, and fight against cholera. We hope in the other round of financing, the primary sector that includes agriculture and its subsidiary, the secondary sector that includes the factory of subcontracting will receive more findings. We based our rationale on the fact that employment created in the first two sectors is more durable and more susceptible to sustain the growth process. In addition, the economic structure of Haiti with a lack of basic infrastructure such as roads, bridges, ports, Airports cannot assure a durable growth build in the tertiary sector.

While everyone in Haiti had a true hope in that organization, a brief note to the media announced the closing of the IHRC. No bilan has been published about the success or failure of that temporary organization. Were all the funds used or not? They were Haitians as well as foreigners leading the IHRC. Since the announcement of the closing, it is a complete silence about that entity. Furthermore, the Clinton-Bush funds officially ended its activities in Haiti by December 2012.

NEW HOPE IN THE MINING SECTOR

The new waves of poverty created by the January 2010 earthquake do not appear to diminish any time soon. However, recently the office of mining in Haiti has reopened the books in that sector. They want to look again at past geophysical searches undertaken in various parts of Haiti. At that time, drilling has indicated the presence of oil and gas and oil. Some oil reservoirs were located in marine sediments between 7000 to 8000 meters deep in the canal of la Gonâve and specifically in the Bay of Rochelois of the Ile of la Gonâve.

Other potential areas of interest include the Central Plateau, the land area of the Plaine du Cul-de-Sac and Great Cayemites. "The current state of knowledge accumulated in the oil potential of Haiti is satisfactory enough to attract investment." But they do not have the technology to exploit the oil in Haiti and relieve the misery of the Haitian people.

In 1949, the Government of Dumarsais Estime had attempted to exploit the oilfields in Haiti using the "Atlantic Refining Company" (ATRECO). The drilling was carried out with the assistance of the Ministry of Agriculture and Natural Resources and Rural Development under the supervision of the agronomist Jean David. They said that if one goes to the town of Caradeux between the International Airport and Pétion-Ville, you can see the traces of Derricks who worked in the area. The mouth of the well is sealed with a copper plate bearing the date of drilling and the name of the ATRECO.

Then, a formal order was given by the responsible of the company to stop work immediately, ATRECO was compensated. Haitian oil farewell!

In 1975, the government of Jean Claude Duvalier called the Crux Limited for the exploration of these resources identified in the oil harbor of Port-au-Prince near the island of la Gonâve and Grande Saline. The Jean Claude Duvalier regime was looking for a way to keep that economic growth they had going on at that time.

The INAREM or National Institute of Mineral Resources managed by Henri P.Bayard began research for nearly six months in Port-au-Prince to the Dominican border as possible area of drilling already undertaken by ATRECO in the Plaine du Cul-de-Sac.It would be well on the road that comes from vicinal Caradeux to go to the chapel of St. Mary of Petion-ville.Samples were taken and analyzed in the laboratory of the Bureau of Mines. Engineers have established the existence of an oil slick underwater adjacent to the oilfields of Venezuela (the capacity of the aquifer is estimated by some 5 times higher than that of its continental neighbor). Once again, the Crux Company Limited was forced to abandon exploration, for the same reasons qu'ATRECO in 1949. A few years later, a geological engineer attempted to resume work in concert with the Venezuelan authorities, and without the vigilance of the Venezuelan police, he would have been killed.

In addition, the former President of the Dominican Petroleum Refinery (REFIDOMSA), Leopold Espaillat Nanita, explained that one of the solutions for the Haitian government to get out of this endless external debt, but also to solve its socio-economic problems, would be in the exploitation of gold deposits as well as other minerals owned by the neighboring territory of the Dominican Republic. Espaillat Nanita revealed that geological studies and research conducted on Haitian soil indicate that this nation has jointly with Saint-Domingue, possibly untapped gold field the largest in the world. Similarly, there is a field (second after South Africa, the leading global provider), a little known ore: Iridium, used in the construction of spacecraft, tactical missiles and other gear. Both resources are sufficient to alleviate "poverty" of the Haitian people.

Espaillat Nanita, who is also an architect, denounces the fact that these resources are not well known because some multinationals, want to remove their natural wealth to the Haitians.

CHAPTER VIII

Can international aid rescue Haiti?

W hile visiting Haiti Franklin Delano Roosevelt asked a selected public audience on how he could help Haiti? The answers were unanimous: end the occupation. Haiti was born following a violent uprising, the only alternative left to the slaves by theirs masters who used them like animals with harsh treatments. Our ancestors were at the forefront of the fight for freedom to end the exploitation by white men. This tendency toward heroism will be transferred from generation to generation. Proponents of ending the American occupation as early as possible, lead by Joseph Jolibois and Stenio Vincent won against those who wanted to deal with the occupants piloted by Sudre Dartiguenave and Louis Borno. The last two have run the country hoping to find the best ways to exploit the technological advances of the occupants.

Years after the American left Haiti, in 1941; the international community began looking at the Haitian case. An export-import Bank was created with the intents to promote the plantation of caoutchouc in Haiti. A lot of plantations were destroyed to be replaced by caoutchouc. This culture failed and many lands became unusable. From 1944 to 1947, the interamerican foundation for education and rural development wanted to help Haiti. Technical schools were created all around the country in the follow-

ing years until 1969. The World Bank and the UNICEF gave loans
to Haiti up to 10.5 million USD. From 1950 to 1970, we received
an average of 4 million dollars annually from several sources. Upon
the arrival of Francois Duvalier, the relationship with our powerful
neighbor turned in the wrong direction. They stopped aiding the
country as retaliation of Duvalier repression against intellectuals.
After the death of Duvalier, the relationship with the two countries
reshuffled again. The American Ambassador in Haiti, Clinton Knox
took part in the succession of Duvalier. Following the taking of oath
of Baby Duvalier, the Americans open their wallets to Haiti. During the first two years of Jean Claude, Haiti received a substantial
amount of aid. Through the end of 1973, the World Bank counted
the international aid to Haiti at $ 15.85 per capita. The Canadian
followed the path of the American and started helping Haiti. Their
help was more technical. They trained agents for the Haitian Public
Administration. They sent professors to the Haitian Universities,
specially the faculty of Agronomy and the National Institute of
Haiti for Management and Administration. Their technicians try
to implant economic model in the country. They supported a program called Regional Development of Petit Goave and Petit trou
de Nippes (DRIPP). Since Dumarsais Estime, Haiti has not known
a long period of growth. A relative economic boom was created by
the massive aid that Jean Claude Duvalier's regime has received.
In 1981, the arrival of mass Haitian immigrants on the Floridian
beaches panicked Washington. The Haitian government was forced
to sign a treaty allowing the coast guard to arrest Haitian boats in
Haitian sea. As reward, the government of Jean Claude received
11.5 millions of dollars. After the fall of Duvalier, the American
gave 55 millions of dollars with the condition that their handpicked
Haitian Finance ministry Leslie Delatour apply some deep reforms
in the Haitian economy. Opposition to the Military called it "the
American plan for Haiti ".

Haiti was never a privileged friend for Washington. Compared
to what the American has done in Cuba before Castro, the Dominican Republic or Panama, aid was always distributed in a dropper

to Haiti. The explanation advanced by some economists of the World Bank is the difficulty for Haiti to absorb the quantity of aid. For example, they mention the lack of qualified personal for the management of project in Haiti. Furthermore, in many cases the Haitian government could not finance its part in the projects.

INTERNATIONAL AID & POLITICAL INTERFERENCE IN HAITI.

According to an old saying, there is nothing new under the sun. Since the emergence of The United States of America as Super power, their diplomacy has not changed: carrots and sticks. In the time of cold war and the Cuban revolution, Haiti had a strategic importance for the United States. They feared a propagation of the Castrism in the Caribbean considered as their backyard. It is in such context, one must analyze the financial aid accorded to Jean Claude Duvalier. As soon as they realized the regime was shaky and the threat of an uprising closed, they forced their client to leave. In addition, the mass exodus of Haitian toward the highly touristic beaches of Miami panicked the conservative and racist sector of America. We have to remember that Haitians are blacks and their revolutionary past was never welcome in the American Empire.

Historically, Americans have always considered the Haitian State as very suspicious in spite of past relationship. There was some period of tension in the relation between the two countries. For example, the 19 years of occupation left Haiti profoundly divided in racial segregation. At each period of tension, the State Department does not hesitate to apply the big stick. From Woodrow Wilson to Barack Obama, every American President has something with the tiny Negro State. These days the united States lead the world as the only superpower. The international aid to Haiti takes the direction of the American vector.

In 1990, Us Vice President Dan Quale arrived in Haiti to insult the military and urged them to organize the election. The General Herard Abraham obeyed. On December 16, 1990 the election put a leftist to power. His anticapitalism is not a secret for Washington. On February 7, he had sworn in as President. Among his guesses a large number of poor people in the town. During the ceremony, he fired the military staff responsible of his security. The American Ambassador warned: After the dance," the drums will become heavy." Aristid responded to him:" hands together are powerful ". After the emotion of the victory and the celebration, Jean Bertrand Aristide had to deal with the reality of poverty in Haiti. The international aid and the foreign investors were not in a hurry to come to the rescue of the government. Amid confusion and division between Aristide and his old allies, the machine guns of Raul Cedras shut up the democratic attempt in the night of September 30, 1991.The international aid was stopped and a general embargo was imposed upon the country under a military junta. During three years the embargo reduced the country GDP almost to half. Meanwhile, the olds friends Aristid and Preval stand in their refusal to talk, the economic sanction destroyed Haiti's economy: 140.000 jobs were lost forever.

OCTOBER 15, 1994: SECOND INVASION OF HAITI.

From his exile in Washington, Aristide built up a political machine to fight for his return. He succeeded to convince the leaders of the Democratic Party and the black caucus to invade Haiti in order to chase Raul Cedras. In the middle of his agenda, Bill Clinton decided to satisfy the black leaders. The black vote counts a lot in the night of election. Moreover, some analysts advance humanitarian reason to justify the new invasion of Haiti. In spite of the opposition of the CIA, Clinton decided the invasion. Raul Cedras and his accomplice were expulsed from the country. The international aid was restored immediately. Like Aristid did in December 1990 with the FNCD, his party wanted to come back to the concession made in Washington. He fired all the army personal and replaced them by a new police force. He refused to allow economic reforms that he had agree to adopt once reinstated. Washington put the pressure on him and he was forced to organize a new election where his trusted man Rene Preval was elected easily. Preval and Aristide enter in conflicts because the former wanted to follow the economic plan neo-liberal required by the International Monetary Fund. Aristide response was to create a new political party with only closed fans. In the following confusion, Prime Minister Rony Smart resigned. The international aid was held waiting for a new prime minister to be installed. Political murders increase suddenly in the country. A new election was held on November 2000, and Aristide sworn as President in February 2001. This time Aristid and Preval became truly political enemies. Aristid could never end any of his political tenure as president of Haiti. Each time he is in the National Palace as president an atmosphere of civil war is installed in the country. Haiti did not have the chance to see Aristid manage the country because he remained the most popular president ever to be elected. This time, the international community put an unofficial embargo on his government. To substitute to the lack of international aid, the country became a transit place for the drug going to the American market. The George W Bush administration blamed Aristid government of being behind the drug trafficking. When Guy Phillip organized an invasion against Aristid, the Bush Administration looked the other way. On February 29, 2004 ended officially the Aristid epic in Haiti.

An imported Prime Minister from the Diaspora is installed, while the head of Haiti Supreme Court became the President. The Drug Enforcement Administration went behind all the suspected drug bosses of the Aristid administration. Again Haiti was under occupation. This time it was a United Nation force led by militaries from Latin America whose mission is to stabilize the country. While I am writing this book, the Minustah has been there for 8 and ½ years and the political troubles are still going on. Following the departure of Aristide, a new form of violence appeared in the country: the kidnapping. Officially, the members of Aristide party " Fami lavalas" denied any involvement in such form of violence. Under the Gerard Latortue leadership, the international aid has resumed with a new plan prepared in the office of the World Bank in Washington. But the greatest realization of Latortue was the election of Rene Preval in May 2006.

Like it is understandable from the analysis we have made so far, Haiti has lost its sovereignty. Haitian politic has become a function of the donor's countries. Some politicians in Haiti bet on the night of American presidential election. The aid donation changes according to Washington wishes. The losers are the Haitian poor. The Haitian experience has proved that aid suspension or embargo to influence political decision does not solve the conflict. The fact to stop the aid sent a message to the belligerent: obey or you lose the aid. In some cases like in 1991, the guilty leaders do not care about sanctions. They create alternative way to survive, for example money laundering from the drug trafficking. During his second term in 2001, Aristide and the group of 184 refused to negotiate while the economic situation of the country was getting worst. The donor's countries delivered only the humanitarian aid and the remittances from the Diaspora were the surest source of revenue for most Haitians. One can challenge this strategy to stop the charity in order to put pressure on local leaders. Many analysts think the suspension of aid caused sometimes irreparable damages. Whatever the reason to stop the support the donors must realize a strategy to keep sending the floats of aids in remote areas. From our observation, we have deducted a functional relationship between aid and interference in Haitian politic for the last decades:
Aid suspension/ Embargo/ Military intervention= Corruption/ Violence/ Poverty

STRUCTURAL ORGANIZATION AND FAILURE OF THE AID IN HAITI.

Haiti is a country with a tradition of dictatorship. After more than two hundred years of independence, Haiti is a failing state. The way of management and the relation between the branches of the State causes some eternal conflicts. We tried all the system: monarchy, republic, president for life. Now for two decades we are struggling to implant democracy in Haiti. What type of democracy? By intellectual wisdom, I agree that the liberal type of democracy cannot be installed at once in Haiti. The inequality is too wide, the division of class and color has not been resolved yet to allow a democratic society to function properly in Haiti. The chronic political instability scared potential investors. Even in period of peace, the judicial system does not function because of corruption. Our economic elite refuses to invest in the long term. Instead of fulfilling their historical role, today some members of the mulatto elite are trying to take over of the political machine. For more than 60 years, no mulatto has been president of Haiti. For some members of that bourgeoisie closed and united, the economic situation has become worst since their absence to the National Palace. The international community wants to help Haiti, but they must take into account the social reality of this country. While the country has been plunging in the abyss of misery, for the last decades our governments have always put reducing poverty the priority of their agenda.

IMPROVING OUR CAPACITY TO ABSORB THE AID

The public administration in Haiti is not yet able to give the partnership needed by the NGOs. Some international aid agencies like USAID, takes the initiative and goes into the field to implement, execute, and follow some projects. The advanced managerial systems in the donor's countries with strict financial control, transparency and responsibility are not in used in Haiti. In 1996, the government of Rene Preval tried to increase the capacity of the public administration. Specific tasks were assigned to the ministries. In 1998, after evaluation it was revealed that the ministries were unable to guide the aid agencies with a specific strategy for manage the projects. At that time the extenuating circumstances were found in the 3 years of embargo imposed to the military junta. Moreover, the public administration has a problem of absentees. About 10% of the personal of the administration are zombies. More than 90% of the budget goes to the salary of employee. The real agent salaries are so low that it affects their morale and they are set for corruption.

INCREASING ADDICTION TO THE INTERNATIONAL AID.

The budget for the fiscal year 2008-2009 has been voted by the Haitian parliament in June 2009, three months before September, 30 last day of the fiscal period. This lateness was due to the time frame taken by some donor's countries which appeared to be tired of the Haitian case. More than half of Haiti's budget is financed through donations. The Haitian elites seem to be pleased to rely on charity to manage their country. They do not realize without a national effort, international aid cannot remove the country from absolute poverty. The priority of any serious government in Haiti should be to solve the political instability, create a safe environment for investors in order to reduce our dependency from the international charity. For the last twenty years, our leaders have given the impression to satisfy the international community before their constituents. As a result, a vast majority of Haitians survive only on the remittances of the Diaspora and the international donors.

FOR A NEW STRATEGY OF AID IN HAITI.

Like we have written previously, the international aid is used by some countries to put pressure on Haitians during our repetitive political crisis. This form of conditioned aid cannot lead to an economic growth. Furthermore, the lack of coordination among donors creates a space for corruption. Haiti needs another form of aid. During the summer of 2008 four hurricanes crushed the country successively. Without the pity of Venezuelan president Hugo Chavez to allow Preval to use the funds of Petro Caribe, a humanitarian catastrophe would have taken place in Haiti. The firing of Prime Minister Jacques Alexis was the result of the lateness in the international aid. The negative choc inflicted to the Haitian economy at the time of the aid suspension or delay in the distribution provokes some irreversible damages. When the aid is back after a period of interruption, many projects need to be readjusted, and in some cases it will take years to have positive results.

HOW TO MAKE THE AID MORE EFFICIENT?

Haiti is not the only country where international aid has failed so far. The international donors are trying all type of strategy in order to increase the efficiency of the aid. The help should aim at some specific development program. The donor's countries should apprehend the problem of poverty closely. More and more, national sovereignty is an alleged reason evoked by the recipient's countries to reduce the right of entry to some complex corridor of corruption. Between interference and sincere collaboration, there is a line to be respected by the donors. Without this good will of donor's countries, failed countries like Haiti should have become a world disaster. The interminable conflicts still cannot stop. As a result, some donors signal sign of fatigue. In Haiti, the addiction developed toward the aid has become so profound that any pause by donors may result in a catastrophe. Every year the number of new aid recipients augments, meanwhile the availability of resources is decreasing. Consequently, the organizations tend to help where the results are quantifiable. Why pumping money in projects where the failure is quasi certain? The financial statements of projects under the government control are not published periodically; meanwhile the ONGs used transparency and quarterly or yearly results are verifiable.

A new strategy taking into account the Haitian environment should be put to trial. The donor's countries have to consider the fragility of the Haitian democracy. They are obsessed more by the results than by the method to succeed. They have to understand failing states like Haiti is a challenge for the donors.

Through the Caribbean Islands, Haiti makes the difference with its situation of absolute poverty. Until the middle of the 80s, Haiti case was not so desperate. Since the fall of the Duvalier regime, the country rarely enjoys long period of stability. After Aristide was toppled by the invasion of Guy Philippe in February 2004, Gerard Latortue could not control the country; the World Bank has decided to place Haiti under a new category: the Pariah States. The arrival of Preval to the Palace progressively lowers the tension and the daily kidnapping in the country. Once again, some NGOs slowed down the flow of aid to Haiti. As a result, in certain regions of the country some projects had to be closed. The needy population is caught between the NGOs and the government. I suggest that the donors treat each project separately according to a specific agenda. Some countries give the aid they want and not what the recipient countries need. For example, when some governments invite Haitian officials to a meeting for aid, they only give them the direction to follow in order to receive the assist. Agency such as USAID works on their own agenda and does not require the advice of Haitian executive. They reproach the lack of responsibility of some Haitian executives. In addition, such agency evaluates their projects by means of standards used in their own country.

THE CONFESSION OF BILL CLINTON.

Former US president Bill Clinton promised to work to promote food self-reliance in Haiti. He has expressed regrets to have put in place policies that have been harmful to Haiti agriculture and the ability to feed its population. We are working on a new strategy to increase the production of coffee and mangos. Economists who are proponents of an endogenous model of growth are very pleased with that U-Turn of Bill. He has spoken very sadly about the role played by his administration in the exportation toward Haiti of subsidized products, taking advantage of Haitian low custom tariff condition imposed by the IMF and the World Bank. By 1998, Haiti could produce 47% of the rice nationally consumed while today the country barely satisfies 10% of the local market.

The productive capacity in agriculture of the country is threaten by the flood of food sent for humanitarian reason but sold on Haitian market. That was a mistake declared Bill Clinton before a commission of the Senate lead by John Kerry. I have to live everyday with the consequences of the fact that Haiti's capacity to produce rice went down because of what I did. Mr. Clinton described the past policy as an effort to skip the steps of agricultural development and to go straight to industrialization. He recognized the failure of that policy everywhere: we cannot take out the food chain from the production. It is risky for the survival of that country.

I think this is very significant commented Mark weisbrot, co-director of the centre for economic policy research (CEPR) based in Washington, reacting to Clinton declaration. It is very rare that a former president gives his excuses for something he did.

The CEPR has also called the international community to buy all the harvest of rice produced by Haiti during the next two years, which represents 2.35% of the actual total of aid promised.

However, we have to watch that the purchasing at the producer level do not disturb the existing network of distribution, said the CEPR. Fortunately, numerous Haitian farmers are organized in network, or cooperatives. The international donors must work with those organizations and farmers in order to elaborate a plan to buy all the rice produced locally and distributed as food aid.

For Gerald Murray, anthropologist at the University of Florida at Gainesville, who is studying Haiti Agriculture, the distribution of free food is necessary during crisis, but Clinton declaration reflects for him an awareness of conscience of the fact that agricultural economy must be encouraged, and that cannot be done by invading the country with free foods, unless it is bought from local farmers.

I think it is an opening, declared Neil Watkins, director of Action aid USA, speaking of Bill Clinton mea culpa. He has at least attired the attention of the urgent need to change the American policy which has gravely damaged the production of rice in Haiti. We can help to nourish the population by trying to make the help more flexible, which will facilitate the country to be rebuilding in the long term.

THE SEINTENFUS APPEAL.

In an interview published by a Switzerland news paper, the representative of the Organization of America State (OAS), Mr. Ricardo Seintenfus gave his ideas about Haiti. According to Seintenfus, since Jean Claude Duvalier departure, there is a low intensity conflict in the country. The system of conflict prevention does not apply in Haiti. There is no civil war in the country. Haiti is not Iraq or Afghanistan; however the Security Council keeps in Haiti a huge security force after the fall of Aristide in 2004. He thinks the Haitian crisis opposed faction struggling for the power. For him, Haiti is paying the price of being geographically too close to the United States. The superpower maintains Haitians prisoner in their own island. The fear of Boat people explains the United States policy toward Haiti. They absolutely want Haitians to stay in their country.

During more than two hundred years of independence, foreign troop's occupation has alternated with local dictatorship. The sin of Haiti was to become a Free State after a war of liberation. They committed the unacceptable in 1804, a crime against the masters of a world in panic. The west is a colonialist world where wealth is builds on slavery and exploitation of new lands conquered. The news of a general uprising by the slaves in the colony of Saint Domingue gave fear to the super powers of that time. Haiti spent years of isolation on the international scene.

There is a part of Haiti which is turned toward foreign countries. They are trying to make Haiti a capitalist country, an exportation platform for the American market. However, Haiti must stay an agricultural country with usual principle of law. The country does not have public resources to run as a State. In a country where the unemployment rate is almost 60%, it is unbearable to extend a stabilization mission because there is nothing to stabilize. Everything has to be built. Haiti represents a symbol of the international aid failure. Instead of sending troops, they must construct dams, roads; participate in the organization of the State. The United Nation is keeping Haiti on a cemetery peace.

Table showing Haiti dependency to International donations.

Program financing

ACDI	4,054,244,325
AIEA	22,487,220
ALLEMAGNE	145,961,146
BID	693,835,314
BANQUE MONDIALE	2,284,535,287
BRESIL	66,000,000
ESPAGNE	1,534,207,163
FAO	1,063,216
FENU	49,312,195
FIDA	143,995,720
FRANCE	427,765,916
IICA	167,376,000
ONUDI	47,300.00
PNUD	173,800,000
TAIWAN	847,088,750
UNION EUROPEENNE	6,231,892,136
UNESCO	5,389,678
UNICEF	38,259,953
USAID	12,224,336,932
VENEZUELA	1,216,000,000
TOTAL	30327598251.00

CHAPTER IX

Haiti: between a UN protectorate and a NGO republic.

The first US occupation of Haiti (1915-1934) gave us a legacy of noirisme/mulatrisme. The second intervention of 1994 has transformed Haiti as an NGO republic. Using as excuses the corruption and inefficiency of Haiti civil service, donor's nations have channeled their help through nongovernmental organizations. We are agreeing that the NGOs are doing an excellent job in Haiti, but the planning ministry should be able to show them the real priorities of the country.

According to some journalists, the number of NGOs in Haiti is from 3000 to 10000 after the earthquake of January 12, 2010. For Bill Clinton, special envoy of the United Nation in Haiti, this country is second in the World in tern of NGOs. The NGOs have saved the Haitian population after the disaster. As we already mentioned, we could not discern what is being done in the planning ministry. Although, we have to recognize that NGO have more ability than the Haitian government. To avoid the bottleneck of the Haitian public administration, donors give their money directly to NGO because they are assured with a good utilization of the help. For the fiscal year (2007-2008),

USAID has spent 300 millions of dollars with some field organizations. Those projects dispose more money than the Haitian planning ministry. Consequently, this ministry does not possess the ability to develop the human resources necessary to manage the projects given to NGOs. Actually, an important proportion of the Haitian population solicits heir needs directly to NGOs. This is not the planning ministry, which takes initiatives, but NGOs that are offering Haitians what they think is necessary for the country. The young Haitians graduated are looking desperately a job in NGOs because of the rate of salary and they can obtain a visa with facility. Some NGOs programs have nothing to do with the pursuit of economic growth in Haiti. For example, the micro credit industry in Haiti has 300 small lending institutions with 200.000 customers and the amount of loans is near to 100 millions of dollars. However, the Haitian leaders have not yet established a body of legislation for those small financial institutions. In addition, we have to mention that those institutions are funded from external sources. We think that the Haitian government should have a t least a role of supervising the program managed through these organizations. I suggest to the new government the increase of efficiency in order to prove donors its ability to manage funds and fight corruption feared by international institutions. Once the trust established again, donors may start transferring projects to the Haitian planning ministry. In the meantime, the presence of NGOs is crucial for Haiti. The unit responsible for external cooperation inside the planning ministry needs to implement a special policy for NGOs. The elements developed inside the strategic document for poverty reduction can serve the basis to establish a long-term operating plan for any government. The Haitian parliament must create laws to control NGO, especially those working in the financial sector. For example, NGO could be classified according to the service offered; each of them could work closely to the Haitian ministry responsible of the sector.

RESTRUCTURING THE PLANNING MINISTRY.

The new mission of the planning ministry should be to specify the sector where the aid is needed. The executive of that ministry must be able to submit the priorities to NGOS. Many questions regarding the Haitian economy have to be answered inside that ministry. Inside the drawer of that department, one can find lot of documents well written by Haitian and foreigners. In spite of the sophistication of those documents, the failure of international aid in Haiti is obvious. Some of those papers take into account the political instability. Maybe it is time to rethink some projects in function of the Haitian context. The publishing by the planning ministry of the Haitian << poverty map >> seemed to be a good response to persons who have criticized them for their lack of long-term vision. In that document I had the chance to read, there are plenty of data. Only there is an absence of clear proposed solution. The financial management, the bottleneck of the Haitian problems, was not envisaged in that document. Many times, donors accuse Haitians of corruption and mismanagement. Writing plans and method of financial evaluation belongs to the planning ministry. In addition, that ministry should work closely to all donors. A publication of the accounting of that ministry should be done periodically. The information about the coherence of the project must be accessible to the public. The goal of that ministry is to clarify discrepancies existing between the exact quantity of aid received and the amount promised by donors. Jointly with the commerce ministry, the planning ministry must list the priorities needed by the country. Reading the Haitian Medias, I have the impression that the USAID plans more for Haiti than the planning ministry. The projects written by that American agency are so well done that the Haitian government could use them. Let us remind that Michele Pierre Louis did not present a program while accessing to the Prime Minister Job. A few days after, we learned through the news that a < plan Collier > for Haiti has been circulating through the Medias. The Finance and Planning ministry of Haiti have applauded the plan. Who should write economic plan for Haiti? The international aid alone cannot lift up Haiti from poverty. However, if used proportionally in the context of Haiti need, a light could be seen in the tunnel in the long term. Donors tend to impose their point of view to assisted countries. In the Haitian case, our leaders make it easy for them. As a result, some NGOs do not require government consensus. He has been proved sometimes that projects failed due to lack of government collaboration. The government and the community of donors have to work together and not parallel. In addition, I suggest in the future that the planning ministry direct some donors in the rural areas. In addition, a decentralization of the international aid to the province town will be welcome.

IS HAITI THE NEXT UNITED NATION PROTECTORATE?

The absence of patriotism from recent and actual Haitian leaders has become notable. The lack of ability to solve the eternal crisis economic and politic places the country under United Nation and NGO rules. Since the 1994 American intervention to reinstate democracy, the dismissal of the army by Aristide, Haiti has been on a Shaky ground concerning public safety. There was no clear development elaborated by the tenants of the National Palace. Haitians must help rebuild Haiti. In spite of our administrative weaknesses a good development strategic plan could work. The international aid will be a complement of the local initiatives. In 2005, Peter Mc Cay, the foreign ministry of Canada speaking about Haiti said:<<the greatest lesson that the Canadians learned from Haiti in the past is the necessity by Haitians to assume the responsibility to create an agenda to develop their own country >> . However, the reality of the international assistance in the country is different. Donors plan and perform. In some cases local authorities learned about projects through the media. This type of act makes the situation worst. For example in 2009, the government of René Preval wanted to have a unique election in 2010 because of the disaster provoked by the four hurricanes of 2008. A foreign embassy disbursed the money for the election. A rigged suffrage took place without a popular support. Instead of solving problems, the organization of those elections created more. A plot prepared internally and externally to topple Aristide is executed progressively. Let us remind that we were on the eve to celebrate the anniversary of our 200 years of independence. That should have been a reason of pride for all blacks in the world. Instead of celebrating that date as a great event comparable at what Dumarsais Estime did in 1950 for the celebration of Port au Prince 200th Birthday, some fake nationalists and patriots used Guy Philippe to cross the Dominican border heavily armed to crush a legal government. Since then, we are under MINUSTAH control.

HOW TO GET RID OF THE MINUSTAH?

On April 30, 2004, the UN Security Council at its 4961st meeting passed a resolution recommending the installation of a troop of stabilization in Haiti. They affirmed their strong commitment to respect the sovereignty, independence, territorial integrity and unity of Haiti. Moreover, the force will monitor all human rights violations, particularly against the civilian population. They served as advisors to the transitional government to take all necessary measures to put an end to impunity and to ensure the continued protection of human rights. The establishment of a state based on the rule of law and an independent judiciary will be among the top priorities.

During the government of Latortue / Alexandre, the role of MINUSTAH was justified because "after the invasion leading to the departure of President Jean Bertrand Aristide in the country, the actions of groups specializing in the disorder prevented any form of stability. A new phenomenon called "Kidnapping" has cost the lives of many citizens. In addition, women were abducted and huge amount of money were claimed to free kidnapped people. In May 2006, an election was held and Rene Preval won with a political platform called "hope." Many politicians thought that the occupation was over. Nothing happened and since then every year, the Security Council UN renews automatically the mandate of Minustah. Strict compliance with the resolution of the Security Council is expected to complete the presence of this force in the month following the election of Rene Preval. At the beginning of their term, Alexis and René Préval asked timidly to the Minustah to leave. However, the political upheavals that led to the dismissal of Alexis silenced the voices calling for the force to leave.

After the January 12, 2010 earthquake devastated Haiti, they had to rely on Minustah troops to help maintain order in cities. On June 4, 2010, the Security Council adopted a new resolution recognizing that Haiti has suffered significant devastation by the earthquake. They stressed the need for Minustah to continue to focus its work on ensuring security and stability in Haiti. The Security Council demands that Minustah help Haiti in its recovery efforts, and reaffirm the authority of the power to insist on the role of the Government of Haiti in its post-disaster reconstruction Period. In addition, the Secretary-General reaffirms the importance of holding municipal, parliamentary and presidential elections within a reasonable time, advising the government of Haiti to encourage all political parties and stakeholders to work together for this purpose. On March 20, 2011, Michel Martelly was elected president of Haiti. He was sworn in May 14, 2011, and then his prime minister and the government were installed in October 2011. The new president is clear in its intentions to get rid of Minustah and he wants to create a force to replace them after their departure. As of September 30, 2011, Minustah in Haiti had 12,294 uniformed personnel. (8752 soldiers and 3542 police officers, 572 civilians, 1,357 local employees, 238 United Nations Volunteers). The new force proposed by the President Martelly and his staff of only 3,500 uniformed personnel. By subtracting the amount proposed by Martelly among the members of Minustah on the ground, there will be a workforce of 8794 personnel missing in securing the country. The amount is large when one considers that banditry and insecurity is still ongoing in many cities.

In February 2012, Minustah will have eight years in Haiti. His goal continues to be adjusted depending on the situation in the country. Based on this logic, the Minustah in Haiti will remain forever. Absolute poverty and misery of the vast majority of the population has not improved. The call to transform part of the troop's development officers is a great idea. We suggest reducing the amount of troops and a portion of the budget reallocated to train security forces created by the Haitian government. We know for sure that the international community is reluctant to encourage the construction of a new army in Haiti because of what happened in the past with the military. In this case, we believe that the international community and friends of Haiti in the world should encourage an increase in the number of agents of the Haitian National Police (HNP). For example, a police force of 15,000 members with some units trained to defend the national territory would be a great achievement to help Haiti regain its sovereignty.

CHAPTER X

What can Haitian living abroad do for Haiti?

T he word Diaspora is so used in Haiti, that its meaning has become biased. The origin of that expression was used to refer to the Jews that fled from Palestine to become a worldwide nation. The Haitian case is worst because poverty pushes the mass exodus. The Haitian tragedy can be analyzed under the angle of the prediction made by British economist Alfred Malthus. He studied the impact of disequilibrium between population and economic growth. Haitian started moving abroad at the beginning of the 20th century. Historian Roger Gaillard in his book, "The White debark reveals that as the twentieth century started , Haitians have begun moving toward the eastern part of Cuba and later to the border of the Dominican Republic. The abandon of the Haitian agriculture by the leaders of the country left no other choices to the peasants: go away to look for fertile lands to cultivate. Specially, in the town closed to the Dominican border, Haitians peasants went there with their machetes looking for work. While the number of Haitian started growing, resentment made the Dominican peasants think that strangers are stealing their lands. They complained to local authorities against this form of invasion by the Haitian whose colors are black. Dominican dictator Rafael Trujillo ordered a general massacre to clean the border town darkened by the Haitians. Those who emigrated through Cuba were luckier because no massacre took place in Cuba. However, at the end of each sugar season (zafra), Cuban police chased them in order to force them back home. Eventually, the next season they will come back. Under the regime of Francois Duvalier, Haitian professionals were encouraged to leave the country toward Africa. The recently emancipated countries of Africa needed them to fill in their public administration. Another group of Haitian left the country to help build the tourists resorts of Bahamas. The Francois Duvalier regime was so intolerant with the intellectuals, once someone was not agreeing with his political rule; you had to flee the country as soon as possible. Most of them went to Canada, Mexico and the United States. At the beginning of the 1980s, Haitians rushed to Florida. Some small boats were used to the transportation and immigrants from Haitian town like Leogane, Port de Paix invaded the sand of Miami Beach. Some observers affirmed that the arrival of boat people to the beaches of Miami was one of the principal grieves of Washington against Jean Claude Duvalier. They used that pretext to force him to step down to power.

Today the number of Haitians residing in Florida reaches about 1.3 millions according to the last census of 2010. The Dominican Republic, Canada, and the USA are the country of predilection of Haitian fleeing their poverty-ravaged country. The remittances sent by those Haitians represent a large proportion of the Haitian national revenue. In front of the importance economic of the Haitian living abroad, a ministry was created for them. I think that this ministry is part of Haitian tradition of bureaucracy and waste of the small revenue of our poor nation. The money used in the Budget for that department ministerial should be redirected toward Agriculture or the Education Department.

After the election of Jean B Aristide in 1990, many Haitians sold their taxi medallions to go back and invest in their homeland. On September 30, 1991, the Haitian army took over the power by organizing a mass killing. Surprised by the events, these Haitians now used to the political freedom in the USA had to comeback in their welcome lands. I was told the adventure of a Haitian immigrant who succeeded financially in Florida. Like many of them, his dream was to go back in the Island to open a Business. To put his plan in application, he took a second mortgage on the family home. Added to his other source of savings, he returned with about 500.000 USD to accomplish his dream. Five years later, he came back to Florida to rejoin his now indebted family. The only profit he made in Haiti was the incurable disease he contracted. Examples of Haitian bankrupt after their attempt to come back are well known in New York, Miami and Montreal. The economic success of some Haitians abroad cannot be repeated in Haiti without an improvement in the business environment over there. Capitalism, which is the economic model for Haitian living abroad, is different from the one in Haiti. Haitian judicial system is completely corrupted. There is no place for real competition. The credit system is not liberalized. A small group only has access to the money in the Haitian banking system.

More and more Haitian livings abroad are becoming important in the political scene of their country. It is clear that the Diaspora can do something for Haiti revival. Now all Haitian candidates come to make a tour of the principal cities to court the community. In the past, businesspersons and the army used to influence election in Haiti, which allowed them to maintain their privilege. Today the army does not exist anymore, and the businesspersons have lost power.

Haitian living abroad enjoy the access to high technology can be a plus for Haiti. Because of their qualifications, the Haitian abroad tends to impose their views in the political choice in the country. For example, through some phone calls, the Diaspora can influence the outcome of election in Haiti. The true influence of the Diaspora comes from the transfer of money made periodically. Many political factions in Haiti are trying to hold a subsidiary in the Diaspora. I do not agree with the concept of 10th department attributed to the Diaspora. On an administrative point of view, decision maker in Haiti must think about it. What is the difference between the Diaspora ministry and the foreign ministry? What is the role of our ambassadors and consuls abroad? On a financial point of view, the minister of Haitian living abroad represents a waste in our budget financed up to 60% by countries friend of Haiti. In my analysis concerning the modification of the Haitian budget, I recommend the closing of that ministry and some others that I consider as squandering of money so scarce in Haiti. The creation of that minister was part of an attempt by our ruling class of the last 20 years to use the Diaspora politically. Furthermore, the ability of the Diaspora to raise money draw Haitian politician to it. The refusal by the Haitian parliament to vote a law recognizing the double nationality is the proof that Haitians living abroad are being exploited for raising money and political lobbies. We have identified the main source of handicap for Haitian wishing to invest in Haiti:

A) The traditional ruling economic class, which refuses to obey to the exigency of modern capitalism. They tend to invest in the export-import sector. It used to be the defect of all the local bourgeoisie of Latin America. However, today this has changed in those countries. For example, Brazil, Mexico, and even in the Dominican Republic a class of investors indigenous takes the risk locally. These countries accommodated themselves to the modern capitalism. They do not depend only on investments abroad. The Haitian bourgeoisie would rather invest in subcontracting industry instead of putting their money in the agri-businesses. In front of any potential investors in the Diaspora will stand the oligarchy well organized and very strong due to the weakness of our judicial system.

B) The second bottleneck for potential investors from the Diaspora lies in the corrupt Haitian civil service. The inefficient Haitian public administration constitutes one reason of our economic lateness. Graduate from abroad; rarely succeed in this organized anarchy. In spite of political regime change in Haiti during the last 20 years, no important changes took place to modernize that administration. I think sincerely because of so many obstacles, the vast majority of Haitians living abroad has no chance to come back and succeed in Haiti.

Tourism.

Beside of direct investments the Diaspora can make in Haiti, Haitian tourist ministry should exploit this market. All citizens living abroad tend to visit their homeland. Professionals in the business of tourism could organize some charters inside Haiti. Our historical monuments glorifying our past shall attract the Diaspora. For example a season touristic with a 3 period for attracting Haitians abroad:

a) Carnival
b) The summer vacation
c) Christmas time

> During summer time, the celebration of "patron saint" in many provinces could attire visitors from abroad who originally were born in the area. Let us assume that for all the 3 periods, the country attires 3% of the 2 millions Haitian living abroad giving 600.000 visitors. If each visitor or Haitian tourist spends $500, the amount of cash added to the Haitian economy will attend 300 million dollars. If we count, the seasonal job created by the arrival of those tourists the total gain for the economy could reach 350 million dollars.

The double Citizenship

We do not want to get involved in the debate of word: nationality vs. citizenship. We are interested in the removal of all legal barriers preventing the Diaspora to help Haiti. The Haitian oligarchy unwilling to respect competition will not stop their old practice. The refusal by the Haitian bourgeoisie to take more risks in investing in the country constitutes a serious handicap for any economic model for Haiti. The possibility for the Diaspora to invest in the country will be a plus for the small and medium businesses. For example, a credit number linked to the social security could be used for Haitian living abroad wishing to invest in Haiti. Haitian bankers complain often that their principal problem is the debt recovery. In the majority of the cases, an interdiction to leaving the country at the Airport is the surest way to put pressure on a bad debtor. The usage of the social security number can allow Haitian bankers to pursue bad debtors living in the Diaspora. One or two credit agencies could be created in Haiti. Collaboration between credit agencies in Haiti and abroad will facilitate the recuperation of bad debt.

Remittances From the Diaspora

2003	2004	2005	2006	2007	2008	2009	2010
811	932	986	1063	1222	1370	1376	1499

From:		USA	Rep.Dom	Canada	France	Guyane	Venezuela

Source: World Bank website

At the dawn of the twenty first century, capitalism is at its height. Marxism belongs to the past. Since the Soviet Empire imploded, Businesses and freedom keep on extending through the planet. A look at the state of affairs in the world will show us that the countries, which adopted the capitalist mean of doing business, are leading the world. Technological innovation, scientific discoveries, social progress belongs to them. However, one must accept the system with its contradiction: profit must be done by at the expense of the workers. Not everybody is satisfied because 90% of the world income belongs to 40% of investors meanwhile the other 10% must be split among the 60% left. The emergence of economic policy filled with social protection diminishes the effect of exploitation. Maybe we are living a momentum of the capitalist system because the history of the world is still unfolding. The Brettonwoods agreements are still running the world economic relationship. There are some new economic powers out there (China, India, Taiwan, and Corea). All of them are located in Asia, which place that continent ahead in the world production.

`We can state that Haiti was never fully integrated in the capitalist system. The Haitian state was created in the aftermath of a violent revolution. Calamities had forced slaves to revolt against theirs masters. Most of the properties were destroyed, and some historians tell that the Saint Domingue 'sky stayed darkened for years. The leaders of the newly born State could not find a way to distribute the wealth. The fonder was murdered. Haiti was kept away of the rest of the world for years. President Jean Pierre Boyer accepted to pay $ 150 million for our independence. After that, the French accepted to trade with their former colony. The new state will never again be prosperous as Saint Domingue. A huge distribution of land orchestrated under Boyer and Petion government had transformed the old property system; the big ones were divided into small owned and worked by peasant's families to assume their survival. Finally, our powerful neighbor recognized our independence and began commerce with Haiti. Our political instability is used by the State Department to invade Haiti. Under a request made by the first National City Bank, our financial system and our custom were put under control. The construction of a railway failed, and we were forced to pay the money anyway. Marines debarked in broad day light to get the money from the safe of the National Bank of Haiti. The goods things of the Occupation were faded by the color division they left behind them. The new segregation system reached its height

under the government of Elie Lescot. To react to the mulatrisme
, a movement called noirisme was spread under the influence of
Jean Price Mars author of the famous book: The uncle has spoken. Some days of uprisings are called, "the revolution of 1946
"by the winners. Nothing had changed in the structure of power
and in the class struggle; some new black faces occupied the civil
service and the political function.

At the Caribbean level, the economic integration is working. Merchant's capitalism is outdated now. To survive the new
technological environment the firms must adjust. In Haiti, the
January 12, 2010 earthquake will hold us back for years. It will
put in delay in our access to the CSME (Caribbean single market economy). The weakness of our system has been proved.
When Port au Prince is paralyzed, the rest of the country does
not exist.

No province town could help the capital. The flow of refugees
that went there realized that there was no structure to welcome
them. In addition, the earthquake proved the lack of leadership
in Haiti. The population noted the silence of President Preval
during the first moment of the disaster. The massive arrival of
international relief only helped to calm the misery. There was
no national plan to get out of that situation. Many meetings
were organized worldwide and finally a committee to rebuild
Haiti (CIRH) was put in place. We do not know if that is another
institution, which will look quietly at the killing of the Haitian
people with complicity of the elites. In 2010, the earthquake that
proved the fragility of the Haitian economy marked the Haitian
economy. According to some estimates, the economic loss represented 120 % of Haiti GDP for 2009.

However, some Haitian businesspersons have showed their
knowhow because the situation could have been worst.

Almost all the sector of the Haitian economy have directly or
indirectly the negative effects of the earthquake. The commerce
and the manufacture sector have been the most affected. The

industries of subcontract went down by 14.6%., except the garment industry.

The agricultural sector was less affected; it was marked by an increase of 4%.The help from the NGO has saved the situation in Haiti. These organizations have increased their activities by 15% which allowed the country to amortize the effect of the choc.

The gross receipts of the government have increased by 4.5%, the direct investments made up for the lack of local investments, the remittances of the Diaspora have increased by 7%; all of these events have helped the Haitian economy to stay afloat. According to some economists, the Haitian economy should be back in positive zone by 2011. The work of rebuilding financed by the Haitian Finance Ministry or by the international community will guarantee the economic growth of 2011. We are hoping that a good political environment and a good management of the CIRH will help accelerate the process of rebuilding.

I would like to urge the decision makers for the next coming years to think about a model economic proper for Haiti. It is not fair to build and prepare economic models for Haiti in the closed office of Washington, Montreal, or Parish. Although one must recognize donations from these countries are vital for Haiti. They can help us with their advanced technology to modernize the country. A good evaluation of the actual available resources in the country should build a good economic plan. For example, some bad decisions of the 1980s are responsible for disappointments today. The destruction of all the pigs of the peasants, the closing of the Leogane sugar plant and Limonade have contributed to the decrease of agricultural productivity in Haiti. We hope that the newly elected parliament will double-check all decision that will affect the goodwill of the nation.

The comeback of Aristide and Duvalier

After the political turmoil caused by the electoral fraud of November 28, 2010, the situation seemed to deteriorate by the day in the country. On Sunday, January 16 2011, the second round of the elections held in November 28 2010 was scheduled. However, the dispute between the candidates Martelly and Celestin had forced the Provisional Electoral Council to postpone the elections indefinitely. In the afternoon of January 16, the national and international medias announced the news of the year: Jean Claude Duvalier was at the Airport in Port au Prince surrounded by many supporters. On the next day he was arrested by the police and complaints multiplied against him in the offices of the Government Commissioner. The spectrum of a trial of the former president for life enraged his fans and they say it is not possible. Many international organizations for human rights are pressure on the Haitian government to put to trial the former president.

Two months after the arrival of Jean Claude, the voice of Jean Bertrand Aristide was heard, and he wanted to return to the country. On Friday, March 18, 1990, he was able to return home with his family. What will be the consequence of this double return of exiled former presidents on the political situation in Haiti?

The return of two former presidents, one of which was the protagonist of the fall of the other is to strengthen political stability, essential condition for sustainable economic growth during this period of reconstruction. The eternal conflict or "madichon of Haiti>> which we have devoted the first chapter of this book will rebound with more force. The mulatrists and noiriste will continue their undeclared war. The Economic oligarchy will not let go because it will continue to enjoy the complicity of our neighbors. As we tried to demonstrate, the Haitian masses are condemned to poverty. Our elites tear each other for control of political power to ensure their personal wealth. Our dependence on international charity is increasing day by day. The last round elections were held in the country March 20, 2011. Already we can augur that the new elected president Michel Martelly will not be able to do anything without a real national consciousness. The elites of this country must understand that it is their own. It is the modernization of our socio-political structures, which has to be considered. We must create a rule of law in which justice must have the upper hand on impunity and corruption. Besides, of the physical reconstruction to replace what the shock of January 12, 2010 has destroyed, one must expect that the civil society will renegotiate a new social contract. Otherwise, this will be the end of this country as a sovereign entity.

NOTES

I)

After the death of Francois Duvalier, the United States of America wanted to give him a reward posthumous for being a fence against the expansion of Fidel Castro ideology in The Caribbean basin. The American ambassador in Haiti Clinton Knox was directed to plan the succession. In order to maintain stability and continuity, Duvalier 'son was designated to replace his father. Baby doc sworn in and declared that he will win the economic battle after the political victory of his father.

With the help of the American government, the capacity energetic of the island received a bust with the construction of a new electric power plant. A five-year plan to augment the agricultural productivity was elaborated. A new industrial park was built near the Airport to lower transportation costs. All taxes on export were eliminated. From 1971 to 1974, about 40.000 jobs were created with a pick of 100.000 around the year 1984. Haiti was second behind Mexico in the exportation of craft and apparels products through the American market. The low salary attracted many investors. The absence of organized unions was also a big advantage for the factory owner.

In spite of a good start, the "economic revolution" of Jean Claude Duvalier failed.
A) The concentration of all the power in Port-au-prince. The newly created industrial park resulted in a savage immigra-

tion of people from the countryside to the capital. The building of one or more industrial park in the North or the center of Haiti would have resolved the problem

B) The government economists had not given full priority to the agricultural plan. Some traditional exports products such as coffee, sisal, cocoa, and vetiver were tumbling down.

C) In spite of the low salary and the lack of unions, some investors refused Haiti without justifying the reason.

D) Growing inflation reduced the purchasing power of the new working class

E) The political conflicts inside the regime where the father in law of the president was accused of encouraging smugglers.

II)

The first military occupation of Haiti could have succeeded. Under the Monroe doctrine, American executives were encouraged to do so in Latin America and the Caribbean. Let us remind that at the beginning of the twenty first century the young emerging industrial power needed market for his products. Protectionism was part of the economic strategy at that time. After a military occupation by the marines, Wall Street bankers took over the financial system of the occupied country. In Haiti, the capitalist met a lot of resistance because of the nature feudalist of the system. That occupation divided the country in two clans.

A) Those who liked the occupation were a large part of the mulatto elite. Only mulattoes were elected president during the occupation. The black feudal bourgeoisie was behind the occupants also. Proponents of the occupation wished to benefit of the technological advance of the American. They were urging the Americans to help them rebuild the infrastructure destroyed during the independence war.

B) On the other side, those called nationalists who opposed the occupation categorically organized a guerilla against the occupants. For them our pride as a free country was down with the presence of foreign troops in our streets. A group of writer called indigenous gathered around Jean Price Mars inspired proponents of that side. In spite of the defeat of Charlemagne Peralte, the marines could not pacify the country. American troops were harassed on a continuous basis. The reinstatement of the "corvee" provoked direct skirmishes between the marines and the peasants. The bilan of the occupation is mixed. They helped stabilize the country. We could finish the payment of the loan to France. The emergence of mulatrisme and noirisme opened a huge hole in the Haitian society leading to the January 1946 uprising and the September 1957 election of Francois Duvalier who will dominate all the institution of the Haitian society.

III)

The reconciliation between the two Haitian elite preached By Mr. Ligonde during the wedding ceremony of Jean Claude and Michelle Bennett had begun long time ago. As soon as Jean Claude Duvalier took office in 1971, many mulattoes returned to Haiti. Inside the agenda of the noiristes fans of Papa Doc, a glimpse to those elite could attire the good will of Washington. Some symbolic changes took place with the firing of some powerful macoute such as Zacharie Delva, Astrel Benjamin, and Adherbal Lherisson. Moreover, Baby Doc's entourage was full with young and attractive women mulattoes

IV)

After the false alarm of Duvalier Departure on January 31, 1986, a savage repression took place in the streets of Haiti. News has spread that a list of young people were about to be arrested soon. For every denunciator, the government will reward a Pajero Mitsubishi. However, Washington did not change his intents. On Wednesday, Neville Gallimore arrived in Haiti from Jamaica. The Washington envoy resided in a motel at the Grand Street of Port au Prince to avoid the wave of foreign journalists arriving in Haiti. Everything went very fast and Baby Doc fled the country at dawn on Friday morning. Even his servants inside the palace did not know anything.

V)

The comeback of Aristide in 1994 was conditioned. Aristide in Washington signed many papers. The lavalassiens supporters did not care about the contents of the papers; Aristide in Haiti was their goal. It sounds like a miracle, because no president could ever return to power after a coup. Shortly after his installment, Aristid was in conflict with his Prime Minister Smark Michel about the deal signed in Washington. Everyone knows that the international community was tired with Aristide hesitation. Finally, Smark Michel resigned and there was a repression against the members of the old Haitian army. Many were killed in the streets or inside their home.

VI)

Michele B Duvalier surnamed by popular mischief << Azoukinking >> or the woman with<< big Glasses>> opened a charity. She built housing, health center, and hospitals. Her image was blemished after she organized a fund raiser of $500.00 per person. The per capita income of Haiti was $340/year; therefore, the majority of the population thought that the first lady exaggerated.

VII)

During a radio interview with Serge Baulieu of Radio Freedom, Roger Lafontant mourned the fall of the Duvalier's regime. He declared he would never forget Claude Raymond and Williams Regala for their betrayal of the duvalierism. Observers remarked he had not mention the name of Henry Namphy, the head of the Government National Council.

VIII)

Many proponents of noirisme in Haiti got married with a colored woman. Salomon married a French woman, Dumarsais Estime; Francois Duvalier had married mulatto's women. Jean Price Mars and Louis Joseph Janvier married ` white women. Is the color question in Haiti a Bluff?

IX)

From 1960, the brutal regime installed by François Duvalier generated serious consequences for the Haitian economy .The clandestine recruitment of cane cutters to the Dominican Republic has expanded and the number officially recruited seemed a joke compared to the illegal from all regions of Haiti. Duvalier encouraged the mass emigration of professionals and technicians from various branches to the United States, Canada, Latin America, Europe and black Africa. In 1960, an entire class of graduate nurses left the country to Canada and the United States. Engineers, economists, professors, doctors, lawyers from Haiti, invaded the newly independent countries of Africa.

X)

In the year 1967, a conflict opposed the two Duvalier sons in law: a black lieutenant of the presidential guard, Max Dominique, and Luc Albert Foucard, a mulatto. Faune Saint Victor, personal secretary who spent hours every day in the office of papa Doc., organized a plot. An electrical mal function put the Palace in the dark. Panicked by the situation, papaDoc run the alarm of the Palace and the Macoutes came to his recourse. He thought an attempt to kill him just failed. He did wait one day and the repression started. A young officer Hilaire, brother of the Palace chaplain had to type the list of person to be arrested. Papa Doc indicated him name after name. The list was up to 18 when the president asked him to stop. He ordered him to add his own name in order to complete the list. The poor Hilaire obeyed and was executed on June 18, 1967.

XI)

In 1843, Jean Jacques Acau led a peasant uprising. Armed with pike, they invaded Port au Price. They claimed to have their own property from the State. Their manifest was: Poor mulattoes are black and rich black are mulattoes. Today a poor mulatto is called ti rouj.

XII)

Roger Lafontant was a powerful member of the militia duvalierist. As Haitian consul in Montreal, he stayed away of the mainstream power in Port au prince. In 1980s, he came back and took power close to the president. His popularity was so high among members of the public administration, the army, and the militia that the president for life watched his movements in the palace yard. Sent into exile by Michele B Duvalier before the collapse of the regime, he reentered the country in 1990 to organize the Duvalier's camp for the election. After the Vertaillis meeting, he became their candidate. The article of 291 of the new Haitian constitution did not allow former Members of the Duvalier's regime to take part in the coming elections. Upset, on January 6, 1991 he took some armored vehicles, entered the palace, and made a speech to cancel the result of the December 16, 1990 election. Arrested, jailed, and put in trial on July 29, day of the VSN, he died mysteriously during the September 30 coup against Aristide.

XIII)

The first political decision of the National Council of Government (CNG) was to dissolve the Para military group named National Security Volunteers (VSN) in the early morning of February 7 1986. In the streets, Macoutes were chased and killed. Many of them were victims of the necklace torture.

Later during the CNG management, to facilitate the vote of the 1987 constitution, the constituents had to insert the article 291, which claimed that macoutes must stay out of electoral contest for ten years. In the public administration, macoutes were fired upon denunciation that someone once saw them in the blue denim uniform. After the failed coup of Roger Lafontant on January 6, 1991, for days macoutes were killed and burned through the country.

The general Henry Namphy, head of the National Council of Government had a split character. He had a reputation of a military and not a politician. However, after a foreign tour, he held a press conference at the Airport, and he sworn that serious things were about to begin now. It was in the month of October 1987. Two weeks after a serial act of vandalism occurred in the capital. In the night after the selection of candidates for the upcoming November election, suspicious fires broke all around the country. Moreover, after that the country will be the scene of many acts of destruction attaining their peak in the morning of the massacre at Valliant Street, on November 29, 1987.

LISTING OF HAITIAN PRESIDENTS.

Jean Jacques Dessalines	1804 - 1806	Assassinated
Henri Christophe	1807 - 1820	Suicide
Alexander Pétion	1806-1818	Died in power
Jean Pierre Boyer	1818 - 1843	Overthrown
Rivière-Heard	1843 - 1844	Overthrown
Philippe Guerrier	1844 - 1845	Died in power
Jean Louis Pierrot	1845 - 1846	Overthrown
Jean Baptiste Riche	1847 - 1847	Died in power
Faustin Soulouque	1847 - 1859	Overthrown
Fabre Nicholas Geffrard	1859 - 1867	Overthrown
Sylvain Salnave	1867 - 1869	Executed
Saget Nissage	1870 - 1874	completed term
Michel Domingue	1874 - 1876	Overthrown
Canal Boisrond	1876 - 1879	Overthrown
Lysius Felicite Salomon	1879 - 1888	Overthrown
François Légitime	1888 - 1889	Overthrown
Florvil Hyppolite	1889 - 1896	Died in power
Tirésias Simon Sam	1896 - 1902	completed term
Alexis Nord	1902 - 1908	Overthrown
Antoine Simon	1908 - 1911	Overthrown
Cincinnatus Leconte	1911 - 1912	Died in power
Tancrede Auguste	1912 - 1913	Died in power
Michel Oreste	1913 - 1914	Overthrown
Oreste Zamor	1914	Overthrown
Daimler Theodore	1914 - 1915	Overthrown
Vilbrun Sam	1915	Assassinnated
Sudre Dartiguevave	1915 - 1922	Completed term (1st US Occupation)
Louis Borno	1922 - 1930	Completed term (1st US Occupation
Eugene Roy	1930	Completed term (1st US occupation)
Sternio Vincent	1930 - 1941	Completed term (occupation until 1934)
Elie Lescot	1941 - 1946	Overthrown
Franck Lavaur	1946	
Dumarsais Estima	1946 - 1950	Overthrown
Paul Eugene Magloire	1950 - 1956	Overthrown
Joseph Nemours Pierre-Louis*	1956 - 1957	Transitional
Franck Sylvain*	1957	"
Collégial	1957	"
Antonio Thrasybule Kebreau (Chairman of the Military Council)	1957	"
François Duvalier	1957 - 1971	Died in power
Jean-Claude Duvalier	1971 - 1986	Fled the country
Henri Namphy	1986 - 1987	Transitional
Lesli Manigat	1988	Overthrown
Henri Namphy	1988 - 1989	Overthrown
Prosper Avril	1989 - 1990	Overthrown
Etha Pascal-Trouillot*	1990 - 1991	Transitional
Jean-Bertrand Aristide (I)	1991	Overthrown

Joseph Nerette*	1991 - 1994	Transitional
Emile Jonassaint*	1994-1994	Transitional
Jean-Bertrand Aristide (II)	1994 - 1996	Completed term
René Préval	1996 - 2000	Completed term
Jean-Bertrand Aristide (III)	2000 - 2004	Overthrown
Boniface Alexandre*	2004 - 2006	Transitional
René Garcia Préval	2006 - 2011	Completed term
Michel Martelly	2011-	

Bibliographie

Al Burt

Bernard Diederich

1969-Papa Doc et les Tontons Macoutes. La verite sur Haiti. New York. McGraw Hill,19

Alejandro Portes

Carlos Dore-Cabral

Patricia Landolt

1997- The Urban Caribbean. Transition to the New Global Economy. The John Hopkins University Press.

Amy Wilentz

1990- The rainy Season. Haiti since Duvalier. Touchstone. Simon & Schuster Building. 1230 Avenue of the Americas. New York. 10020

Banque Centrale de la République d'Haïti.

Département des Etudes Economiques.. Bulletin de la Banque de la République d'Haïti.(Octobre 1993 et 1994

Carlo Desinor

1986. Daniel Fignole. Un espoir vain. Port au Prince. L'imprimeur.1986

Gérard Pierre Charles

1987- Radiographie d'une dictature. Port au Prince. Le Natal.1987.

Hans Schmidt:

1971. The United States occupation of Haiti (1915-1934) Rutgers University Press. New Brunswick, New Jersey.

Terry f.Buss:

2008. Haiti in the balance. Why Foreign Aid has failed and what we can do about it. National Academy of public Administration. Brookings Institution Press

Hilbourne A Watson:

1994.The Caribbean in the Global political Economy. Lynne Rienner Publishers Inc. New York, 1994.

Joseph E. Stieglitz:

2002. Globalization and its Discontents.W.W Norton & Company.

Kern Delince

1979. Armée et Politique en Haïti. Paris; L'harmattan, 1979.

Lundal, Mats:

1979. Peasants and poverty: A study of Haiti. New York. St Martin Press.

Lyonel Paquin

1986- Classes sociales en Haïti: Classe moyenne et super classe. New York. L Paquin 1986.

Michel Rolph Trouillot:

Haiti, State against Nation. The origin and legacy of Duvalierism.Monthly review press.122 west 27th street.

New York, New York 10001

Michele Wucker

1999- Why the cocks fight. Dominicans, Haitians, and the struggle for Hispaniola. Hill & Wang. A division of Farrar, Strauss and Giroux. 19 Union Square West, New York 1003

Muhammad Yunus:

2007-Creating a World Without Poverty. Social Business And the future of Capitalism. Public Affairs. New York

Noam Chomsky

Paul farmer

Amy Goodman

2004- Getting Haiti right this time. The US and the coup. Common Courage Press. 112 Red Barn Road. Monroe, ME 04951

Robert Calderisi

2006-The trouble with Africa. Why Foreign Aid isn't working Palgrave Macmillan. 175 5th Avenue, New York 10010

Roger Dorsinville

1980- Mourir pour Haïti ou les croisées d'Esther. Paris. L'harmattan. Collections Encres Noires. 1980

Roger Gaillard

1982- Les blancs débarquent: Hinche mise en croix. Port au Prince. Le Natal,1982.

1982-Les blanc debarquent:Charlemagne Peralte, le caco. Port-au Prince. Le Natal,1982.

1983-Les blancs debarquent:La guérilla de Batraville. Port au Prince. Le Natal 1983.

Simon Fass:

2004- Political Economy in Haiti. The drama of survival.

Transactions publishers, New Brunswick, New, Jersey

Steven D. Levitt

Stephen J. Dubner

2005-Freakonomics. A rogue Economist explores the hidden side of everything. Publishers Harper Collins

WWW.brh.net

www.RadioTelevisionCaraibes.com

WWW.lenouvelliste.com

www.mef.guv

WWW.mpce.guv

WWW.ihsi.net

Indexes

Cheju

Chimere

China

Christophe

Church

CIA

Citizen

Clan

Class

Coastal

Cocoa

Code

coffee

coffee

Colon

Colony

Color

Colorist

Columbus

commercial

Community

Competition

Complexity

Comprehension

concession

Conflicts

Construction

Contacts

Contrast

Convention

Coordination

Corruptin

Corvee

Coverage

Credit

Crime

Culmination

Cumberland

Curve

Customs

Cycle

Damages

Damiens

Daniel

Data

Debate

Debile

Debt

Decade

Decades

Deficit

Degrading

Dejoie

Democracy

Democratic

Demography

Department

Deregulation

Design

Diagnosis

Diaspora

Diaspora

Dictator

Dimemnsion

Diplomatic

Discrepancy

disobedience

Dividends

Documents

Dollars

Dominican

Donations

Dumarsais

Duvalier

Earthquake

Economic

Education

Elite

Embargo

Emotion

Employment

End

Endemic

Endogenous

England

Ennemies

Enterprises

Environment

Equality

Erosion

Eternal

Europe

Events

Exclusive

Executive

Exile

Exorbitant

Exploitation

Export

Farnham

Favorable

Fight

Finance

Financial

Fiscal

Food

Forest

Fraction

Fragment

France

Funds

General

Generation

Geography

Globalization

Government

Greve

Group

Growth

Haiti

Hans

Hemisphere

Henry

Heritage

High

Hispagnola

Hispagnola

Historian

History

Human

Ideology

Impartial

Imperial

Impertinence

Import

Important

Incompetence

Independence

Industries

Inequality

Inflation

insecurity

Institution

Intense

International

Invasion

investments

Investor

Irrigation

Irrigation

Island

Jean

Jobs
Justice
Lack
land
Lavalas
Law
Leogane
Leslie
level
Liberal
liberalisation
Macoute
Magloire
Majority
Manifestation
Manufacturing
Many
Marine
Market
Mass
Massacre
Members
Mercantile
Michel
Migration
Miles
Military
Minister
Ministry
Mission
Model
Modernization
monarchy
Monetary
Money
Month
Mountains
Mulatrism

Mulatrist
Mulattoes
Mutation
Nation
National
Never
NGOs
Noirisme
Number
Occupants
Occupation
Order
Organisation
Package
Palace
Panama
Panorama
Paris
Parity
Parliament
Patriotism
Payment
Peace
Peasants
Pedagogue
Period
Perpetual
Phenomenon
Pierre
Plan
Planet
Plantation
Plateau
Pole
Police
Policy
Politics
Population

Population
Populist
Port au Prince
Port au Prince
Poverty
Power
Precept
Presidency
Press
Primary
Primordial
Private
Problem
Production
Production
Productive
Productivity
Progres
Projects
Projects
Property
Protectorate
ProvincesPopulation planning
Public
Race
Raul
Reason
Reforms
Regime
Relationship
Religion
Republic
Reserves
Ressources
Restructuring
Resultats
Revenue
Revolt

Revolution
Rivalry
role
Saint Domingue
sanctions
Scale
School
Sector
Security
Simultaneous
Situation
Slavery
Small
social
Sovereignty
Spain
Spanish
Specialist
Stability
State
StepSeitenfus
Strategy
Streets
System
Taxes
Teacher
Technology
Term
Think
Thought
Time
Title
Too
Tourism
Tourists
Traditional
Troops
Under

Us

Venezuelan

Very

Victory

Wages

Wars

Way

Which

White

Workers

World

Year

Zones

www.ingramcontent.com/pod-product-compliance
Lightning Source LLC
Chambersburg PA
CBHW070647290526
45790CB00001B/207